**AMERICAN HISTORY** Begin

# myWorld
## INTERACTIVE
### Active Journal

# SAVVAS
## LEARNING COMPANY

Savvas Learning Company LLC, 15 East Midland Avenue, Paramus, NJ 07652

Cover: Tall Ship Festival - shaunl/Getty Images

Attributions of third party content appear on page 232, which constitutes an extension of this copyright page.

ISBN-13: 978-0-328-96504-5
ISBN-10:     0-328-96504-9

12 2021

# CONTENTS

# CONTENTS

. . . . . . . . . . . . . . . . . . . . . . . . . . . . . . . . . . . . . . . . . . . . . . . .

## Topic 3
## The Revolutionary Era (1750–1783)

## Topic 4
# A Constitution for the United States (1776–Present)

# CONTENTS

# Topic 5
# The Early Republic (1789–1825)

## Topic 6
# The Age of Jackson and Westward Expansion
## (1824–1860)

# CONTENTS

. . . . . . . . . . . . . . . . . . . . . . . . . . . . . . . . . . . . . . . . . . . . . . . . . . .

## Topic 7
## Society and Culture Before the Civil War
(1820–1860)

# Topic 8
# Sectionalism and Civil War (1820–1865)

# CONTENTS

## Topic 9
## The Reconstruction Era (1865–1877)

# The Early Americas and European Exploration Preview

## Essential Question  How much does geography affect people's lives?

Before you begin this topic, think about the Essential Question by completing the following activities.

**1.** Name three geographical features and how they might influence human activity.

**2.** Preview the topic by skimming lesson titles, headings, and graphics. Then, place a check mark next to the human activities that are directly influenced by geography.

| | | | |
|---|---|---|---|
| __Farming | __Trade | __Singing | __Culture |
| __Dancing | __Navigation | __Exploration | __Sports |

## Timeline Skills

As you read, write and/or draw at least three events from the topic. Draw a line from each event to its correct position on the timeline.

| 500 | 700 |
|---|---|

# Map Skills

Using the map in your text, label the outline map with the regions listed. Then, draw lines to represent the migration of people into these regions based on the land-bridge theory and the coastal-route theory.

Eastern Woodlands     Great Plains          Southeast          Southwest
Arctic/Subarctic      Northwest Coast       California/Great Basin

900          1100          1300          1500

## Quest
### Document-Based Writing Inquiry

# The Easter Mutiny

On this Quest, you need to evaluate the reliability of Antonio Pigafetta's account of the Easter Mutiny. You will examine sources from Pigafetta's time as well as an interpretation of one of these sources by a modern historian. At the end of the Quest you will write a research paper that summarizes your findings.

### 1 Ask Questions (See Student Text, page 6)

As you begin your Quest, keep in mind the Guiding Question:
**How reliable is Antonio Pigafetta's account of the Easter Mutiny?**

What other questions do you need to ask in order to answer this question? Consider how a person's point of view can influence his or her writing and affect our understanding of a person or event. Two questions are filled in for you. Add at least two questions for each category.

**Theme** Purpose

Sample questions:

Why did the author write this document?

How did the author intend this document to be used?

**Theme** Author

**Theme** Audience

**Theme** Origin

**Theme** Bias or Perspective

**Theme** My Additional Questions

 **INTERACTIVE**

For extra help with Step 1, review the
21st Century Tutorial: **Ask Questions**.

## ② Investigate

As you read about the early Americas and European exploration, collect five connections from the text to help you answer the Guiding Question. Three connections are already chosen for you.

## Connect to Mansa Musa

**Lesson 3 In-Text Primary Source** *Catalan Atlas* (See Student Text, page 34)

Here's a connection! Look at the quote in your text from *Catalan Atlas*. How does this quote verify the information in Mansa Musa's biography?

What other type of primary source might verify Mansa Musa's biography?

## Connect to Magellan's Biography

**Lesson 4** 5 Things to Know About Ferdinand Magellan
(See Student Text, page 43)

Here's another connection! What facts from Magellan's biography help you verify facts in Pigafetta's account?

What questions would you ask Pigafetta about his journey with Magellan if you could talk to him?

## Connect to Christopher Columbus

**Primary Source** Christopher Columbus's Diary (See Student Text, page 47)
Do you believe Columbus's account of his journey?

Do the details he provides give credibility to his account?

It's Your Turn! **Find two more connections. Fill in the title of your connections, then answer the questions. Connections may be images, primary sources, maps, or text.**

## Your Choice | Connect to

### Location in text

What is the main idea of this connection?

How does this connection help verify related primary sources?

## Your Choice | Connect to

### Location in text

What is the main idea of this connection?

How does this connection help verify related primary sources?

## ③ Examine Primary Sources (See Student Text, page 48)

Examine the primary and secondary sources provided online or from your teacher. Fill in the chart to show how these sources provide further information about the Easter Mutiny. The first one is completed for you.

| Source | What this source tells me about the Easter Mutiny . . . |
|---|---|
| Pigafetta's Account of the Easter Mutiny | Members of Magellan's crew rebelled against him but were stopped by Magellan. |
| Interpretation of a Modern Historian | |
| The Log of the Pilot of the *Trinidad* | |
| Report to King Charles from His Secretary Maximillianus Transylvanus | |
| Report of the Mutiny by a Portuguese Historian | |

👆 INTERACTIVE

For extra help with Step 3, review the 21st Century Tutorial: **Analyze Primary and Secondary Sources**.

## ④ Write Your Essay (See Student Text, page 48)

Now it is time to put together all of the information you have gathered and use it to write your essay.

1. **Prepare to Write** You have collected connections and explored primary and secondary sources. This will help you understand how sources can be used to verify information in other sources. Look through your notes and choose the evidence you will use in your essay. Record your evidence and sources here.

**Evidence and Sources**

2. **Write a Draft** Using evidence from the clues you found and the documents you explored, write a draft of your response to the Guiding Question: **How reliable is Antonio Pigafetta's account of the Easter Mutiny?** Consider all the evidence and draw your own conclusions. In your essay, be sure to clearly state your view in a strong topic sentence, use logical organization, and support your conclusion with evidence and relevant facts.

3. **Share with a Partner** Exchange your draft with a partner. Tell your partner what you like about his or her draft and suggest any improvements.

4. **Finalize Your Essay** Revise your essay. Incorporate any feedback you received. Correct any grammatical or spelling errors. Use a word-processing program to type a final version.

5. **Reflect on the Quest** Think about your experience completing this topic's Quest. What did you learn about Magellan and his journeys? What did you learn about assessing the reliability of source documents? What questions do you still have about Magellan and his explorations? How will you answer them?

## Reflections

## Take Notes

**Literacy Skills: Summarize** Use what you have read to complete the
table. Include at least one detail from the text for each subtopic listed.
The first one has been completed for you. Then, use the information
you have gathered to create a summary statement.

| Mayas | Aztecs | Incas |
|---|---|---|
| **Environment and Modifications**<br>• Grew enough corn to feed large cities<br>• Made roads between the coast and the inland city-states | **Environment and Modifications** | **Environment and Modifications** |
| **Government**<br>• Each city-state controlled a city and its surrounding area.<br>• City-states battled for land, riches, and trade route access. | **Government** | **Government** |
| **Religion and Culture**<br>• Priests performed ceremonies for harvests and battle victories.<br>• Priests studied astronomy and mathematics and made calendars. | **Religion and Culture** | **Religion and Culture** |

**Summary Statement: How did farming affect early settlers of the Americas?**

 **INTERACTIVE**

For extra help, review the 21st Century
Tutorial: **Summarize**.

# Practice Vocabulary

**Use a Word Bank** Choose one word from the word bank to fill in each blank. When you have finished, you will have a short summary of important ideas from the section.

## Word Bank

terraces    quipus    causeways    city-state

civilizations    surplus    settlements    glaciers

................................................. caused sea levels to fall, uncovering

the land bridge between Siberia and present-day Alaska. This allowed

people to spread across the continent. Eventually people began to

farm, which led to permanent ................................................. . In

time, growing a ................................................. of food allowed the

first cities to form. These cities—along with an organized government,

different social classes, complex religion, and record keeping—gave

rise to new ................................................. in the Americas. The first

were the Olmecs in what is now Mexico. They later influenced Mayas,

who developed the ................................................. , a political unit that

controls a city and its surrounding land. Later, Aztecs formed a

civilization to the northwest with ................................................. ,

or raised dirt roads. Far to the south, Incas also maintained roads,

which teams of runners used to spread royal orders. They carried

................................................. , cords with knots that stood for numbers,

thereby serving as message-recording devices. Incas used engineering in

advanced ways, including creating ................................................. that

allowed them to farm mountainsides.

# Take Notes

**Literacy Skills: Classify and Categorize** Use what you have read to complete the flowchart. Include at least one detail from the text for each subtopic listed. The first one has been started for you.

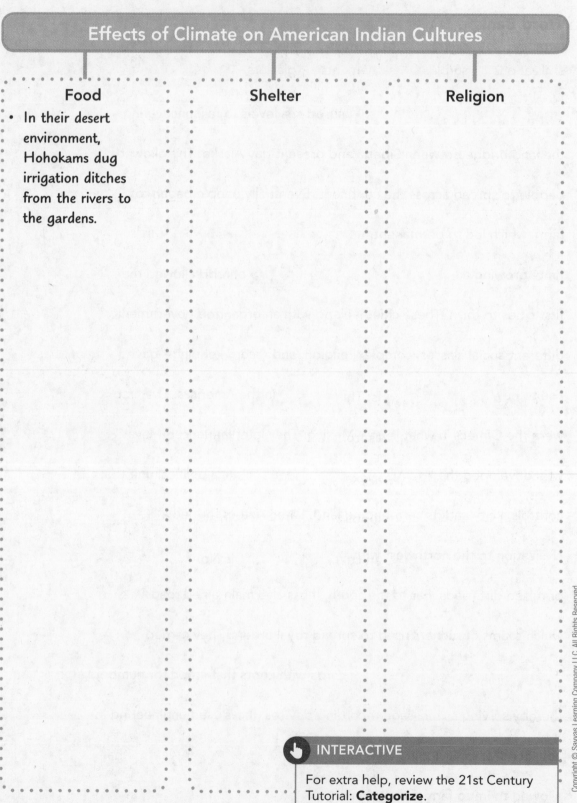

**Effects of Climate on American Indian Cultures**

**Food**
- In their desert environment, Hohokams dug irrigation ditches from the rivers to the gardens.

**Shelter**

**Religion**

**INTERACTIVE**

For extra help, review the 21st Century Tutorial: **Categorize**.

# Practice Vocabulary

**Use a Word Bank** Choose one word from the word bank to fill in each blank. When you have finished, you will have a short summary of important ideas from the section.

## Word Bank

culture     diffusion     tribe     potlatch     adobe

Pueblo     Iroquois League     clan     culture region

A ........................... is the way of life of a group of

people. Most cultures have a distinct style or type of home, clothing,

economy, arts, and government. For example, the Anasazi, called

........................... (meaning village) Indians by the Spanish,

built homes with ..........................., or sundried brick. A

........................... is a large area where people share a lifestyle.

A ........................... is a community of people that shares common

customs, language, and rituals. Through ...........................,

the process of spreading ideas from one culture to another, skills, such as

farming, were exchanged. For example, you may have been to a potluck, or

a communal meal with food supplied by the people in attendance. A similar

even occurs in American Indian cultures of the Pacific Northwest during a

ceremonial dinner called a ........................... American Indian

families from this region host these dinners to improve social standing by

sharing food and gifts. An example of governmental unification is with

the Iroquis. A ........................... is a group of related families.

In the 1500s, the original five nations formed an alliance, known as the

..........................., to end the frequent wars with each other.

## Quick Activity Matching Game

Draw lines to match each American Indian culture in Column 1 with the corresponding fact about its climate, resources, or lifestyle in Column 2.

| Column 1 | Column 2 |
|---|---|
| Hohokams | 1. built large buildings with walls of stone and adobe |
| Anasazis | 2. played games on ballcourts |
| Hopewells | 3. were nomads who followed the buffalo |
| Inuits | 4. used redwood trees to build houses and canoes |
| Yoruk | 5. made earth mounds for religious ceremonies |
| Natchez | 6. religious leaders prayed to kachinas for good harvests |
| Iroquois | 7. women held political power, owned property, and did most of the farming |
| Sioux | 8. used seal-oil lamps and made waterproof boots from seal skins |
| Pueblo | 9. used calendars with 13 months named after foods they harvested and animals they hunted |

Team Challenge! Create a matching game with sets of cards using the name of an American Indian culture on one card and the facts about its climate, resources, or lifestyle on the other. Play your game with a partner.

# Take Notes

**Literacy Skills: Summarize** Use what you have read to complete the flowchart. Include at least one detail from the text for each subtopic listed. The first one has been completed for you. Then, use the information you have gathered to create a summary statement.

| Effects of Increased Trade on Renaissance Leaders | Effects of Increased Trade on Renaissance Exploration | Effects of Increased Trade on Renaissance Scholars |
|---|---|---|
| • Trade brought new prosperity, which increased rulers' power.<br><br>• In England and France, kings and queens worked to bring powerful feudal lords under their control.<br><br>• In Spain and Portugal, Christian monarchs drove out Muslim rulers, who had governed there for centuries. | | |

**Summary Statement:** What was the impact of increased trade on the European Renaissance?

**INTERACTIVE**

For extra help, review the 21st Century Tutorial: **Summarize**.

## Practice Vocabulary

**Words in Context** For each question below, write an answer that shows your understanding of the boldfaced key term.

1. In European **feudalism** in the Middle Ages, how was the role of lord defined in relation to a monarch?

2. What is a technological **innovation** that traveled from the Muslim world to Europe, and what benefit did it bring?

3. What trade routes became known as the **Silk Road**?

4. In what sense was **kinship** central to many ways of life in early Africa?

5. How did the invention of the **astrolabe** help sailors?

6. How did feudal life evolve around the **manor**?

7. During the **Crusades**, who were the Christians fighting against, and why were they fighting?

8. What was the **Renaissance**?

# Take Notes

**Literacy Skills: Identify Cause and Effect** Use what you have read to complete the chart. Draw a line connecting each cause to its effect. The first one has been completed for you.

| Cause | Effect |
|---|---|
| 1. King Ferdinand and Queen Isabella financed Columbus's voyage west across the Atlantic to reach the East Indies. | Almost half the world's food crops come from plants that were first grown in the Americas. |
| 2. Portuguese sailors pioneered new routes around Africa toward Asia in the late 1400s. | The monarchy of Spain paid for the cost of new exploration because it wanted the riches that might be discovered. |
| 3. American Indians introduced Europeans to valuable produce. | Within 100 years, the Taino population was almost wiped out by European diseases and harsh conditions imposed by colonizers. |
| 4. Europeans introduced domestic animals from Europe and Africa. | The crew of the *Niña*, *Pinta*, and *Santa Maria* changed course and approached land. |
| 5. A flock of birds flew southwest over Columbus's ships. | American Indians learned to ride horses and to use them to carry heavy loads. |

👆 INTERACTIVE

For extra help, review the 21st Century Tutorial: **Identify Cause and Effect**.

# Practice Vocabulary

**Word Map** Study the word map for the word *colony*. Characteristics are words or phrases that relate to the word in the center of the word map. Non-characteristics are words and phrases not associated with the word. Use the blank word map to explore the meaning of the word *circumnavigate*. Then make word maps of your own for these words: *turning point* and *Columbian Exchange*.

**Characteristics**
occupation, settlement, foreign

**Definition in your own words**
settlement initiated by a government to occupy new territory

**colony**

**Non-characteristics**
unintentional, assimilation, welcomed

**Picture or sentence**
Columbus founded the first Spanish colony in the Americas.

**Characteristics**

**Definition in your own words**

**circumnavigate**

**Non-characteristics**

**Picture or sentence**

# Quick Activity Dinner Party

Plan a dinner party using items from the Columbian Exchange.
Make a list of ingredients to include in the dinner. These ingredients
must be foods that American Indians introduced to Europeans or
that Europeans introduced to American Indians. Make another list
of activities and conversation topics to entertain your guests.
These must relate to the skills exchanged by Europeans and
American Indians, and to the negative and positive impacts of the
Columbian Exchange.

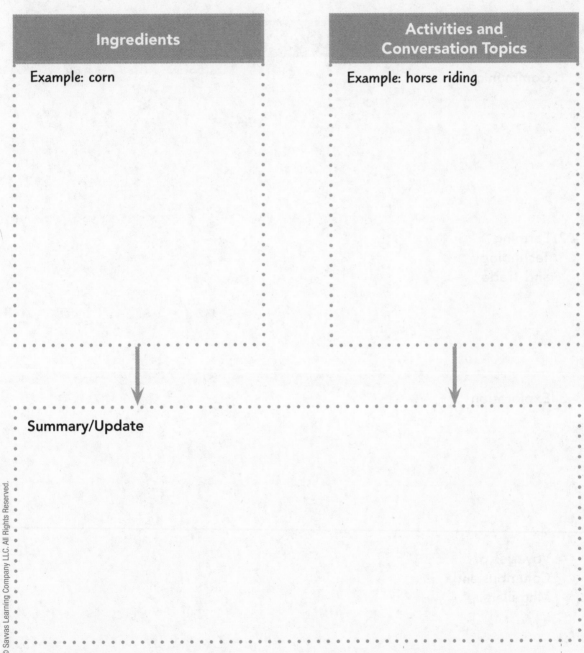

| Ingredients | Activities and Conversation Topics |
|---|---|
| Example: corn | Example: horse riding |

Summary/Update

**Team Challenge!** Write a summary/update about the results of your Columbian
Exchange dinner party. Share your summary with a partner.

# Writing Workshop Research Paper

As you read, build a response to this question: **How did a travel-related invention or improvement in the 1400s or 1500s affect exploration and trade during this time period?** The prompts below will help walk you through this process.

## Lessons 1, 2, 3, and 4 Writing Tasks: Generate Ideas
(See Student Text, pages 13, 24, 38, and 46)

For each lesson, record details about the impact of travel-related inventions on the peoples of North America.

| Lesson | Impact of Travel-Related Inventions on . . . |
|---|---|
| 1. Communication | |
| 2. Farming Technology and Trade | |
| 3. Exploration | |
| 4. Voyages of Columbus and Magellan | |

## Lesson 3 Writing Task: Develop a Clear Thesis (See Student Text, page 38)

Choose a travel-related invention or improvement that you learned about in this topic. You will write about your choice in your research paper. Based on your selection, write an introduction to your research paper in which you clearly state your thesis. Your thesis should address the question: How did a travel-related invention or improvement in the 1400s or 1500s affect exploration and trade during this time period?

## Lesson 4 Writing Task: Find and Use Credible Sources
(See Student Text, page 46)

Identify three credible sources of information you could use to write your research paper. You will use this information to conduct research and to cite the evidence you collect from these sources.

## Writing Task (See Student Text, page 49)

Using the thesis you wrote, answer the following question in a five-paragraph research paper: How did a travel-related invention or improvement in the 1400s or 1500s affect exploration and trade during this time period? As you write, be sure to support your ideas with evidence and cite sources. Use a word-processing program to produce and publish your research paper.

# European Colonization of North America Preview

## Essential Question  Why do people move?

Before you begin this topic, think about the Essential Question by completing the following activities.

**1.** List three reasons why people in your community, or someone you know, may have moved.

**2.** Preview the topic by skimming lesson titles, headings, and graphics. Then, place a check mark next to the ideas that may have prompted Europeans to move to the Americas.

__ luxury

__ make money trapping animals

__ conquest of land

__ study Indian languages

__ practice religion freely

__ glory and gold

__ become a monk

__ more say in government

__ search for a passage to the Far East

## Timeline Skills

As you read, write and/or draw at least three events from the topic. Draw a line from each event to its correct position on the timeline.

| 1500 | 1550 | 1600 |
| --- | --- | --- |

# Map Skills

Using the map in your text, label the outline map with the places listed. Then, color the water blue and use other colors to shade the regions of Spanish, French, and British territories.

| | | |
|---|---|---|
| Middle Plantation | St. Augustine | New Amsterdam |
| Charles Town | Quebec | Mississippi River |
| Roanoke River | Savannah River | Plymouth |
| Baltimore | Philadelphia | New Orleans |

1650          1700          1750

**Quest**

Project-Based Learning Inquiry

# Examining the Colonial Environment

On this Quest, you are part of a group in England that must decide where to become colonists in the Americas. You will examine sources from this period to help you learn more about how previous colonists lived and thrived in their environments. At the end of the Quest, you will create a digital portfolio that includes maps, charts, and other visuals so the group can see how the physical environment has influenced the economy and population across the colonies.

## 1 Ask Questions (See Student Text, page 54)

As you begin your Quest, keep in mind the Guiding Question: **How did the environment influence the economy and population of the British colonies?** Also, consider the Essential Question: **Why do people move?**

What other questions do you need to ask to answer these questions? Consider the following aspects of the physical environments in the colonies. Two questions are filled in for you. Add at least two questions in each category.

**Theme** Water and Natural Resources

Sample questions:

What role did water and other natural resources play in the locations of colonial settlements?

How did water influence the ease and frequency of trade?

**Theme** Farming, Agriculture, and Industry

**Theme** Society, Arts, Ideas, and Education

**Theme** Government and Warfare

**Theme** My Additional Questions

**INTERACTIVE**

For extra help with Step 1, review the 21st Century Tutorial: **Ask Questions**.

## 2 Investigate

As you read about the British colonies, collect five connections from your text to help you answer the Guiding Question and understand how the colonists made a living. Three connections are already chosen for you.

## Connect to the Environment

**Lesson 3** How Did People Live in the Towns of New England?
(See Student Text, page 88)

Here's a connection! Read the section titled The Environment Influences Economic Activity. In what ways was the environment helpful to people looking to make a living?

In what ways was the environment a challenge?

## Connect to the Middle Colonies

### Lesson 4  Daily Life in the Middle Colonies (See Student Text, page 96)

Here's another connection! The Middle Colonies were extremely successful. How was the environment there more favorable than in New England?

What impact did the environment have on the economy and population?

## Connect to Tidewater and Backcountry

### Lesson 5  How Did Two Regions Develop Differently?
(See Student Text, page 106)

What does this connection tell you about how a worker would benefit from living in the Tidewater?

How would a worker benefit from living in the backcountry?

It's Your Turn! **Find two more connections. Fill in the title of your connections, then answer the questions. Connections may be images, primary sources, maps, or text.**

## Your Choice | Connect to

### Location in text

What is the main idea of this connection?

What does this tell you about how the environment influenced the economy and population of the colonies?

## Your Choice | Connect to

### Location in text

What is the main idea of this connection?

What does this tell you about how the environment influenced the economy and population of the colonies?

## ③ Conduct Research (See Student Text, page 126)

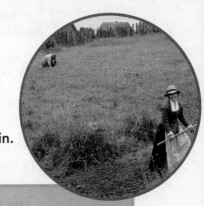

You will need to conduct research on maps, graphs, charts, and/or models that describe the physical environment, economic activities, and population distribution of the colonies. Use the chart below to organize your sources and understand your data. Be sure to include source citations so that you can find them again.

| Source Citation | Description |
| --- | --- |
|  |  |
|  |  |
|  |  |
|  |  |
|  |  |

👆 **INTERACTIVE**

For extra help with Step 3, review the 21st Century Tutorials: **Read Charts, Graphs, and Tables**; **Read Physical Maps**; and **Read Special-Purpose Maps**.

## 4 Create a Digital Portfolio (See Student Text, page 126)

Now it's time to put together all of the information you have gathered and use it to create a digital portfolio so your group can make informed decisions.

1. **Prepare to Write** You have collected connections and explored primary and secondary sources that contain maps, graphs, charts, and/or models that describe the British colonies' geographical features, natural resources, and industry. Use the chart to synthesize your information by region. Then, create your digital portfolio based on your teacher's instructions.

The Environment and the Economy

| New England Colonies | Middle Colonies | Southern Colonies |
|---|---|---|
| Geographical Features | Geographical Features | Geographical Features |
| Natural Resources | Natural Resources | Natural Resourcse |
| Industry | Industry | Industry |

2. **Write a Recommendation** In your introduction paragraph, address the relationship between the geography, economy, and population distribution for each region. For focus, use the Guiding Question, the Essential Question, and your digital portfolio. In the body, outline the portfolio contents and the main points each piece conveys. Conclude with recommendations for settlement location and the role each person in the settlement will assume.

3. **Make Group Decisions** Each team member will make a five-minute portfolio presentation. As a group, compare cover letters to identify similarities and differences. Develop consensus on as many issues as possible. Determine the order of your presentation, ensuring that each person is presenting some element of the digital portfolio. As a group, end your presentation with your team's recommendations, including differing viewpoints team members may have on issues that didn't have consensus.

4. **Reflect on the Quest** Think about your experience completing this topic's Quest. What did you learn about the environment and its effects on the British colonies? What questions do you still have? How will you answer them?

**Reflections**

INTERACTIVE

For extra help with Step 4, review the 21st Century Tutorials: **Identify Trends**, **Analyze Data and Models**, and **Support Ideas with Evidence**.

# Take Notes

**Literacy Skills: Summarize** Use what you have read to complete the table. Write two or three sentences that summarize each major idea. Then, combine them to form a summary of the chapter. The first one has been completed for you.

| Conquistadors and Exploration | Colonization and Settlement of New Spain | Transatlantic Slave Trade |
|---|---|---|
| The Spanish wanted gold and glory, and explorers were required to send one-fifth of their treasure back to Spain. Some of the reasons they conquered the Aztecs and Incas included superior weapons, disease, and fighting between the two empires. | | |

**Summary**

**INTERACTIVE**

For extra help, review the 21st Century Tutorial: **Summarize**.

# Practice Vocabulary

**Sentence Builder** Finish the sentences below with a key term from this section. You may have to change the form of the words to complete the sentences.

## Word Bank

conquistador     pueblo     presidio     mission

peninsular     Creole     mestizo

1. Settlements made up of people whose goal is to convert others to Christianity are called

2. People of mixed Spanish and Indian background are known as

3. People who were born in Spain and were at the top of the social ladder in the Indies were known as

4. A Spanish word for *conqueror* is

5. Those born in America to parents of Spanish origin are known as

6. The towns in Spanish settlements were called

7. Soldiers lived in forts with thick, high walls called

## Take Notes

**Literacy Skills: Sequence** Use what you have read to complete the chart. Sequence three to five events that led up to the formal establishment of colonies for the French, Dutch, and English settlers. The first event has been entered for you.

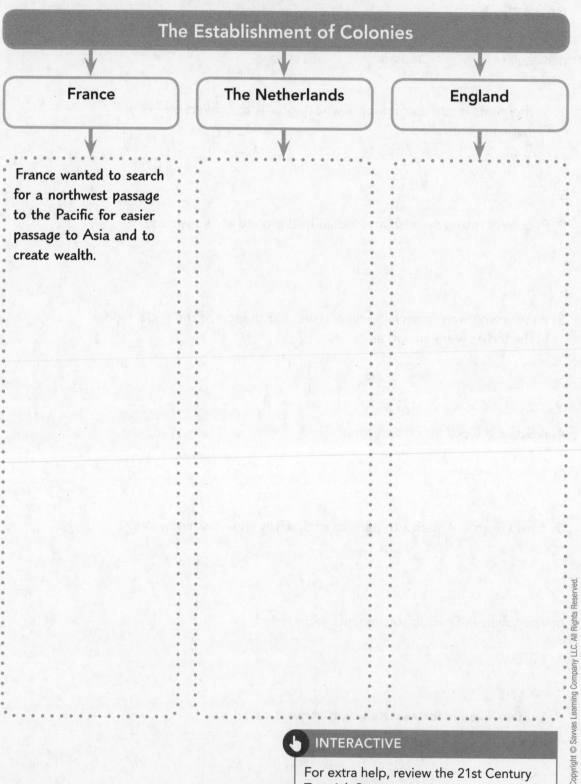

### The Establishment of Colonies

| France | The Netherlands | England |
| --- | --- | --- |
| France wanted to search for a northwest passage to the Pacific for easier passage to Asia and to create wealth. | | |

👆 INTERACTIVE

For extra help, review the 21st Century Tutorial: **Sequence**.

# Practice Vocabulary

**Words in Context** For each question below, write an answer that shows your understanding of the boldfaced key term.

1. Which country established a **representative government** in Virginia, and what does it mean to have one?

2. What are **alliances**, and why were they important for the colonists?

3. What was the **northwest passage**?

4. What are **charters**, and how did they influence the establishment of colonies?

5. Who were the **coureurs de bois**?

6. What happened during **Bacon's Rebellion**, and what were the consequences?

7. What is a **burgess**, and what is its significance?

# Take Notes

**Literacy Skills: Compare and Contrast** Use what you have read
to complete the chart. Compare and contrast the formation of
government in the New England colonies. Include in your notes how
religion influenced the development and changes in each colony. The
first one has been completed for you.

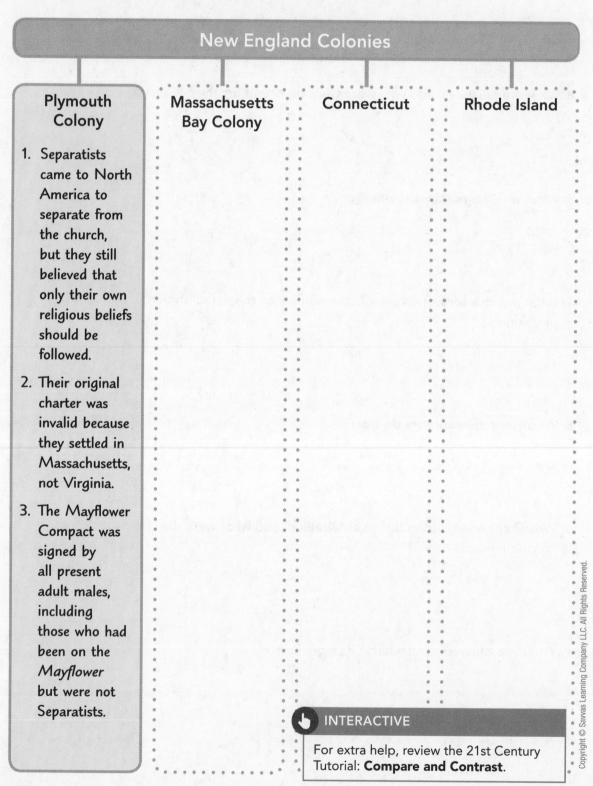

## New England Colonies

### Plymouth Colony

1. Separatists came to North America to separate from the church, but they still believed that only their own religious beliefs should be followed.

2. Their original charter was invalid because they settled in Massachusetts, not Virginia.

3. The Mayflower Compact was signed by all present adult males, including those who had been on the *Mayflower* but were not Separatists.

### Massachusetts Bay Colony

### Connecticut

### Rhode Island

👆 **INTERACTIVE**

For extra help, review the 21st Century
Tutorial: **Compare and Contrast**.

# Practice Vocabulary

**True or False?** Decide whether each statement below is true or false. Circle T or F, and then explain your answer. Be sure to include the underlined vocabulary word in your explanation. The first one is done for you.

1. **T / F** The Pilgrims were Separatists who founded the colony at Plymouth.

   True; The Pilgrims wanted to separate from the Church of England and won a charter to set up a colony in northern Virginia.

2. **T / F** Religious tolerance is a willingness to let others practice their own beliefs.

3. **T / F** The Mayflower Compact was a type of bag brought onto the *Mayflower* to keep track of personal belongings.

4. **T / F** At town meetings colonists discussed and voted on issues that were important to their communities.

5. **T / F** The General Court was a court designed to solve problems in Rhode Island.

6. **T / F** Puritans did not want to separate entirely from the Church of England. They wanted to simplify worship by eliminating practices inherited from the Roman Catholic Church.

7. **T / F** Persecution is when people are honored because of their religious beliefs.

# Quick Activity Write a Letter

Imagine that you are a Pilgrim preparing to get on the *Mayflower*.
Write a letter persuading other Separatists to join you on the journey
across the Atlantic Ocean.

**Team Challenge!** In small groups, share your letters. Who do you
think was more persuasive? What do you think made the arguments
stronger?

# Take Notes

**Literacy Skills: Analyze Text Structure** Use what you have read to complete the table. For each main idea, provide two or three supporting details. The first one has been completed for you.

## The Development of the Middle Colonies

| Main Idea | Supporting Details |
|---|---|
| New Netherland became New York. | England wanted New Amsterdam for themselves. Dutch governor Peter Stuyvesant was unpopular, and the colonists refused to help him, so the English won without a fight. King Charles II of England gave New Netherland to his brother, the Duke of York, and it was renamed New York. |
| New Jersey formed out of New York and became a royal colony. | |
| Pennsylvania was established as a model of fairness. | |
| The middle colonies thrived. | |

**INTERACTIVE**

For extra help, review the 21st Century Tutorial: **Support Ideas with Evidence**.

# Practice Vocabulary

**Matching Logic** Using your knowledge of the underlined vocabulary words, draw a line from each sentence in Column 1 to match it with the sentence in Column 2 to which it logically belongs.

| Column 1 | Column 2 |
| --- | --- |
| 1. <u>Quakers</u> were Protestant reformers who fled persecution in England. | Direct rule from the English monarch tended to be harsh. |
| 2. The Duke of York established New Jersey as a <u>proprietary colony</u>. | They exported so much grain that they became known as the Breadbasket Colonies. |
| 3. The middle colonies thrived largely on <u>cash crops</u>. | They believed that all people were equal and rejected all war. |
| 4. The <u>Pennsylvania Dutch</u> got their name because people could not pronounce the word *Deutsch*. | The king gave some loyal men the land in exchange for yearly payment. |
| 5. New Jersey became a <u>royal colony</u>. | They included the Amish and Mennonites, who liked the idea of people of different religions living peacefully together. |

## Take Notes

**Literacy Skills: Classify and Categorize** Use what you have read to complete the charts. Categorize two to three details from each important element of life in the regions of the Tidewater and the backcountry. Examine how the two regions developed differently. The first detail has been completed for you.

**Tidewater Region**

| Farming | Trade | Daily Life |
|---------|-------|------------|
| Fertile coastal farmland allowed planters to grow crops such as rice, tobacco, indigo, and cotton. | | |

**Backcountry Region**

| Farming | Trade | Daily Life |
|---------|-------|------------|
| | | |

INTERACTIVE

For extra help, review the 21st Century Tutorial: **Categorize**.

## Practice Vocabulary

**Vocabulary Quiz Show** Some quiz shows ask a question and expect the contestant to give the answer. In other shows, the contestant is given an answer and must supply the question. If the blank is in the Question column, write the question that would result in the answer in the Answer column. If the question is supplied, write the answer.

| Question | Answer |
| --- | --- |
| 1. | 1. Act of Toleration |
| 2. | 2. slave codes |
| 3. What is the name of the plant used to make blue dye? | 3. |
| 4. What is the belief that one race is superior to another? | 4. |
| 5. | 5. debtor |

# Take Notes

**Literacy Skills: Summarize** Use what you have read to complete the table. Provide details about each aspect of colonial life. Then, use these details to summarize this lesson. The first one has been started for you.

| Structure | Arts and Education | Religion and Ideas |
|---|---|---|
| Distinct social classes included gentry, middle class, lower class, and enslaved. | | |

**Summary**

**INTERACTIVE**

For extra help, review the 21st Century Tutorial: **Summarize**.

# Practice Vocabulary

**Sentence Revision** Revise each sentence so that the underlined vocabulary word is used logically. Be sure not to change the vocabulary word. The first one is done for you.

1. During the <u>Great Awakening</u>, many colonists totally gave up religion.
   During the <u>Great Awakening</u>, many colonists questioned their religion and changed their beliefs.

2. The <u>Enlightenment</u> was a movement to reject all forms of religion.

3. The <u>Gullah</u> language emerged as a combination of English and Dutch.

4. <u>Libel</u> is when you say something that is true that can damage a person's reputation.

5. <u>Dame schools</u> were institutions where girls could go to live and study.

6. The <u>gentry</u> class included tradespeople and represented the majority of the population.

7. The <u>middle class</u> consisted of people who agreed to work without wages in exchange for passage across the ocean.

8. Sometimes a boy would become an <u>apprentice</u> so he could remain in school his whole life.

# Quick Activity Newspaper Headlines

With a partner or small group, imagine that you are preparing the front page of a newspaper in one of the colonies. Write three headlines that you think would represent the biggest stories of the day.

**Team Challenge!** With your partner(s), select one of your headlines and create an illustration that would go with it. Then, post your illustration and headline to the class board.

**Featured Illustration**

# Take Notes

**Literacy Skills: Draw Conclusions** Use what you have read to complete
the chart. Examine aspects of colonial trade and colonial foundations
of government, and record each topic's details. Draw conclusions about
how both led to a push for colonial independence. The first detail has
been completed for you.

### Trade and the English Colonies

England wanted tight control over
trade with the colonies so that
England would profit the most.

### Foundations of Government

### Conclusions

**INTERACTIVE**

For extra help, review the 21st Century
Tutorial: **Draw Conclusions**.

# Practice Vocabulary

**Use a Word Bank**  Choose one word from the word bank to fill in each blank. When you have finished, you will have a short summary of important ideas from the section.

## Word Bank

| | | | |
|---|---|---|---|
| Yankees | Glorious Revolution | legislature | English Bill of Rights |
| mercantilism | Navigation Acts | export | triangular trade |
| import | bill of rights | | |

The British believed strongly in the idea of ............................. .

They also believed that countries should .............................

more goods than they ............................. to make

a profit. England wanted all the profits of its colonies, so the

............................. was passed so that the colonies could

only trade with England. Merchants from New England, nicknamed

............................., dominated colonial trade. One trade

route known as the ............................. had three points

of contact: New England, West Africa, and the West Indies. As the

colonies started to govern themselves more, elements of government

from England became more important. Many colonies established a

............................., or a representative assembly. In the 1680s,

the ............................. in England resulted in the dethroning

of King James II. Soon after, the ............................. was

signed. A ............................. is a list of freedoms that

the government promises to protect. All of these developments greatly

influenced how the colonies ultimately established a new government.

# Writing Workshop Narrative Essay

As you read, build a response to this prompt: **Write an essay from the perspective of a newly arrived settler in the thirteen colonies.** The prompts below will help walk you through the process.

**Lessons 1 and 2: Introduce Characters** (See Student Text, pages 64 and 77)

Imagine you are a colonist living in North America. Fill in the first row of the chart with your name, your role in society, and two or three sentences describing who you are and what your life is like. Use details from the text. Fill in the second and third rows of the chart for two people your character interacts with. Explain what these people do for a living and how they know your character. You will use this information for a narrative essay you will write at the end of this topic.

| Characters | |
|---|---|
| **Name and Role** | **Description** |
| | |
| | |
| | |

**Lesson 3: Establish Setting** (See Student Text, page 89)

Describe the setting where your character lives in the colonies. Incorporate details from the topic.

## Lessons 4 and 5: Organize Sequence of Events
(See Student Text, pages 99 and 109)

Make an ordered list to show what will happen to your character in
your essay.

## Lessons 6 and 7: Use Narrative Techniques, Descriptive Details, and
Sensory Language (See Student Text, pages 120 and 125)

Brainstorm and fill in the table with other writing elements you may
use in your essay.

| Narrative Techniques | Descriptive Details | Sensory Language |
| --- | --- | --- |
|  |  |  |

## Writing Task (See Student Text, page 127)

Imagine that you are a newly arrived colonist. Use the notes you
made to write a narrative essay, from the perspective of a newly
arrived settler in the thirteen colonies, in which you describe daily life.
Give a detailed account about who you are, who you might interact
with, and what challenges you face.

# The Revolutionary Era Preview

## Essential Question  When is war justified?

Before you begin this topic, think about the Essential
Question by answering the following questions.

1. What are good reasons for going to war? Put a check
mark next to the reasons that you think would prompt
a justifiable war.

___ Too many taxes

___ No voice in government

___ Government cuts off trade with the world

___ Government punishes illegal acts of civil disobedience

___ Government keeps soldiers among the people in times of peace

___ Government forces people to house soldiers

___ Government officers inspect the cargoes of ships for no reason

2. Look at the items you checked. Is any one, by itself, a good enough reason to
go to war? Or would it take more than one of these reasons to justify a war?

## Timeline Skills

As you read, write and/or draw at least three events from the topic.
Draw a line from each event to its correct position on the timeline.

| 1750 | 1760 | 1770 |
| --- | --- | --- |

# Map Skills

**Using maps throughout the topic, label the outline map with the places listed. Then color in the territory claimed by Britain and Spain.**

New Hampshire    Massachusetts    New York    Connecticut

Rhode Island    New Jersey    Pennsylvania    Delaware

Maryland    Virginia    North Carolina    South Carolina

Georgia

| 1780 | 1790 |
|------|------|

### Project-Based Learning Inquiry

# Choosing Sides

On this Quest, you are living in the Chesapeake Bay region in 1776 and must decide whether to become a Patriot, become a Loyalist, or stay neutral in the Revolutionary War. You will gather information about how the region's geography influenced people's views on the conflict by examining sources in your text and by conducting your own research. At the end of the Quest you will write a blog post that documents your decision-making process.

## 1 Ask Questions (See Student Text, page 132)

As you begin your Quest, keep in mind the Guiding Question: **How did colonists decide which side to support in the Revolutionary War?** and the Essential Question: **When is war justified?**

What other questions do you need to ask in order to answer these questions? Consider the following themes related to the Revolutionary Era. Two questions are filled in for you. Add at least two questions for each category.

**Theme** Historical Factors

Sample questions:

What problems did the French and Indian War cause between Britain and its colonies?

How might the colonists' belief in their rights as English citizens, such as those protected by the Magna Carta and the English Bill of Rights, have influenced their views on the Stamp Act and other British actions in the 1760s and 1770s?

**Theme** Society and Demographics

**Theme** Geography and Economy

**Theme** Land and the Proclamation of 1763

**Theme** Government and Laws

**Theme** My Additional Questions

 **INTERACTIVE**

For extra help with Step 1, review the
21st Century Tutorial: **Ask Questions**.

# Quest CONNECTIONS

## 2 Investigate

As you read about the Revolutionary Era, collect five connections from your text to help you answer the Guiding Question. Three connections are already chosen for you.

## Connect to Chesapeake Region Trade

**Lesson 2** Why Did the Stamp Act Anger Colonists? (See Student Text, page 146)

Here's a connection! Look at the Chesapeake region trade map in your text. Which colonies were in the Chesapeake region? In what way was Britain involved in the economy of the region? What does this map tell you about the importance of trade to the Chesapeake region?

What does this map tell you about why British policies that restricted trade might have angered the people of Chesapeake Bay?

## Connect to Thomas Paine's Ideas

**Lesson 4** What Did Thomas Paine Say in *Common Sense*?

(See Student Text, page 167)

Here's another connection! Thomas Paine was a British-born writer who lived in Philadelphia and tried to encourage colonists to resist the British government and King George III. What does the excerpt from his writing say about the importance of kings compared to ordinary, honest men?

How do you think colonists might have reacted to this argument?

## Connect to *Common Sense*

**Primary Source** Thomas Paine, *Common Sense*

(See Student Text, page 177)

What arguments does this connection offer to those who were deciding whether to support the Patriots or Britain? Thomas Paine's pamphlet was distributed throughout the colonies. Was he a Patriot or a Loyalist? What does Paine have to say to those who felt an obligation to the king?

According to the essay, why did Britain offer help and protection to the colonies?

It's Your Turn! **Find two more connections. Fill in the title of your connections, then answer the questions. Connections may be images, primary sources, maps, or text.**

## Your Choice | Connect to

### Location in text

What is the main idea of this connection?

What does it tell you about how the colonists decided which side to support during the Revolutionary War?

## Your Choice | Connect to

### Location in text

What is the main idea of this connection?

What does it tell you about how the colonists decided which side to support during the Revolutionary War?

# ③ Conduct Research (See Student Text, page 190)

Form teams based on your teacher's instructions. Meet to decide who will create each segment of your blog. In the chart below, record which team member will perform which task.

You will research further only the segment that you are responsible for. Use the ideas in the connections to further explore the subject you have been assigned. Pick who or what you will write about, and find more sources about that subject.

Be sure to find valid sources, and take good notes so you can properly cite your sources. Record key information about your area of research here.

JOIN, or DIE.

| Team Member | Segment | Specific Topic of Segment |
|---|---|---|
| Historical Factors | | |
| Society and Demographics | | |
| Geography and Economy | | |

👆 INTERACTIVE

For extra help with Step 3, review the 21st Century Tutorials: **Work in Teams, Search for Information on the Internet,** and **Avoid Plagiarism**.

## 4 Create Your Blog (See Student Text, page 190)

**Now it's time to put together all the information you have gathered and use it to write your segment of the blog.**

1. **Prepare to Write** You have collected connections and explored primary and secondary sources that tell you about the Chesapeake Bay region during colonial times. Look through your notes and decide which facts would help you decide whether to be a Patriot, Loyalist, or neutral colonist. Record them here.

2. **Write a Draft** Decide as a team which side of the war you will support. Then write a draft of your segment of the blog, explaining how your assigned theme affected your team's decision. Include any maps or images that might help illustrate your position. Be sure to include evidence that you have gathered and citations for the evidence used.

3. **Share with a Partner** Once you have finished your draft, ask one of your team members to read your draft and provide comments on the clarity and flow of the information. Revise the segment based on his or her comments, and comment on his or her segment, if possible.

4. **Put Together Your Blog** Once all team members have written and revised their segments, it's time to put them together. As a team, discuss how you will organize your information. Be sure to write smooth transitions from one segment to the next and finish with a strong conclusion.

5. **Present Your Blog** Present your completed blog to your classmates as a group. Listen to the other teams' blogs, and take notes on the information they shared using a separate sheet of paper.

6. **Reflect on the Quest** After all the presentations, discuss your thoughts on your blog and the other blogs. Reflect on the project and list what you might do differently next time so the teamwork goes more smoothly.

**Reflections**

 INTERACTIVE

For extra help with Step 4, review the 21st Century Tutorial: **Give an Effective Presentation**.

# Take Notes

**Literacy Skills: Sequence** Use what you have read to complete the flow charts. Each box contains a specific event, and the boxes are placed in the order in which events happened. The first one has been completed for you.

### George Washington and the French and Indian War

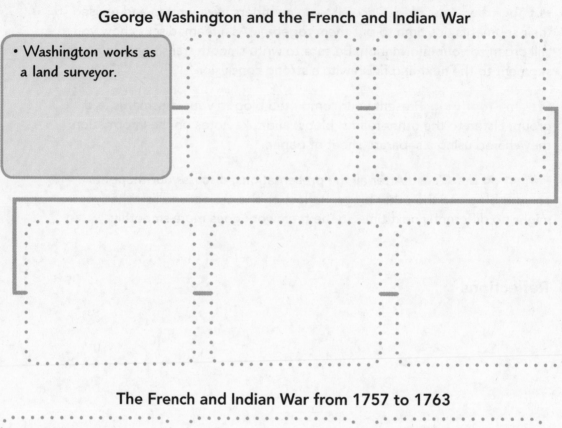

- Washington works as a land surveyor.

### The French and Indian War from 1757 to 1763

**INTERACTIVE**

For extra help, review the 21st Century Tutorial: **Sequence**.

# Practice Vocabulary

Word Map Study the word map for the term *French and Indian War*.
Characteristics are words or phrases that relate to the word or words in
the center of the word map. Non-characteristics are words and phrases
not associated with the word or words. Use the blank word map to
explore the meaning of the term *Treaty of Paris*. Then make word maps
of your own for these terms: *ally* and *Albany Plan of Union*.

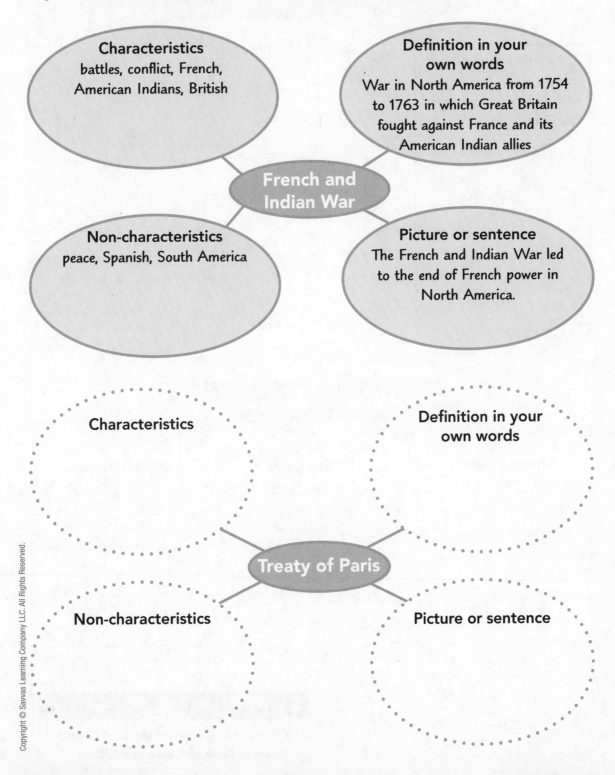

**Characteristics**
battles, conflict, French,
American Indians, British

**Definition in your
own words**
War in North America from 1754
to 1763 in which Great Britain
fought against France and its
American Indian allies

**Non-characteristics**
peace, Spanish, South America

**Picture or sentence**
The French and Indian War led
to the end of French power in
North America.

**French and
Indian War**

**Characteristics**

**Definition in your
own words**

**Non-characteristics**

**Picture or sentence**

**Treaty of Paris**

# Take Notes

**Literacy Skills: Identify Cause and Effect** Use what you have read to complete the charts. The top box contains the effect and the boxes below contain the causes. The first one has been completed for you.

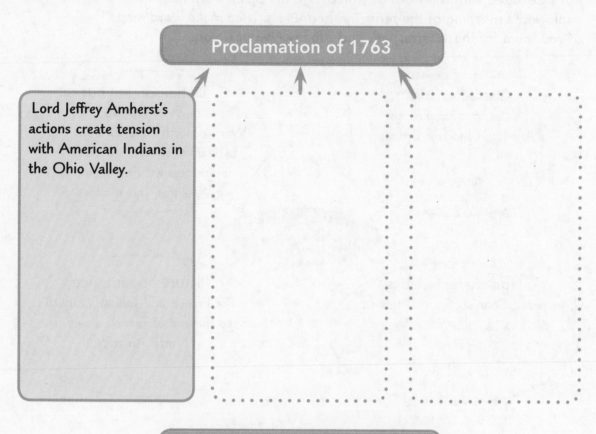

**Proclamation of 1763**

Lord Jeffrey Amherst's actions create tension with American Indians in the Ohio Valley.

**Resentment Against the British**

**British Policies**

**British Laws**

**British Actions**

> **INTERACTIVE**
>
> For extra help, review the 21st Century Tutorial: **Analyze Cause and Effect.**

# Practice Vocabulary

**Sentence Builder** Finish the sentences below with a vocabulary term from this section. You may have to change the form of the words to complete the sentences.

## Word Bank

petition                          boycott                                     repeal

writ of assistance         committee of correspondence

1. A formal written request signed by a group of people is called a

................................................

2. Parliament cancelled the Stamp Act, which means that the act was

................................................

3. Legal documents that allowed British customs officers to inspect a ship's cargo without giving a reason were called

................................................

4. When the colonists refused to buy British tea, they were

................................................ the tea.

5. Colonists who joined letter-writing campaigns to protest British policies were members of a

................................................

## Quick Activity Make a Timeline

With a partner or small group, examine this painting of George Washington during the Battle of Monongahela during the French and Indian War.

### Did you know?

During the war, George Washington learned that American Indian battle tactics were very effective against British troops.

What does this portrayal of George Washington tell you about how he was viewed? How did the French and Indian War lead to conflicts and actions that contributed to the start of the American Revolution?

The Proclamation of 1763

**Team Challenge!** How does this map relate to the causes of the American Revolution? Create a timeline of major events and ideas that led to the American Revolution, such as the ones depicted in these images. Add events and ideas as you read and explain the significance of each. Add some images to help illustrate your timeline.

# Take Notes

**Literacy Skills: Summarize** Summarize the content of the main headings in this lesson using the tables on this page. As you work, pay special attention to the subheadings in the reading. The first main idea has been completed for you.

| The Boston Tea Party | How Did King George III Strike Back at Boston? | The Battles of Lexington and Concord |
|---|---|---|
| **Main Idea:** Colonists protest the Tea Act. | **Main Idea:** | **Main Idea:** |
| **Details:** Parliament kept the tax on tea when it repealed all other taxes with the Townsend Act. The Tea Act of 1773 cut out American merchants from the tea trade. Americans boycotted tea and drank coffee. | **Details:** | **Details:** |

| The Fighting Continues | Opposing Sides at War |
|---|---|
| **Main Idea:** | **Main Idea:** |
| **Details:** | **Details:** |

**INTERACTIVE**

For extra help, review the 21st Century Tutorial: **Summarize**.

# Practice Vocabulary

**Vocabulary Quiz Show** Some quiz shows ask a question and expect the contestant to give the answer. In other shows, the contestant is given an answer and must supply the question. If the blank is in the Question column, write the question that would result in the answer in the Answer column. If the question is supplied, write the answer.

| Question | Answer |
| --- | --- |
| 1. What is the name for colonial volunteers who were ready to fight at any time? | 1. |
| 2. | 2. Loyalists |
| 3. | 3. civil disobedience |
| 4. | 4. Patriots |
| 5. What is the term for an army of citizens who serve as soldiers during an emergency? | 5. |

## Take Notes

**Literacy Skills: Use Evidence** Use what you have read to complete the concept webs. Enter evidence in the outer circles that supports the main idea in the center circle. The first circle has been filled in for you.

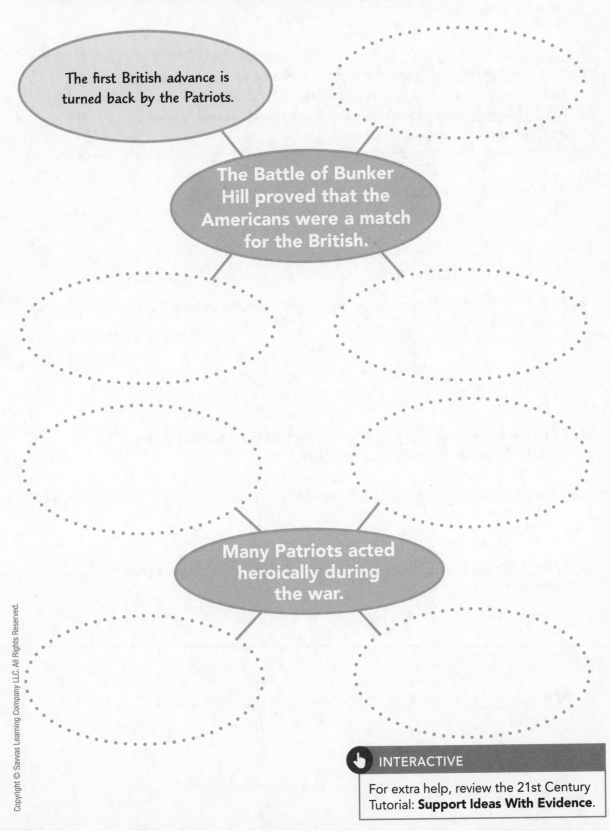

The first British advance is turned back by the Patriots.

The Battle of Bunker Hill proved that the Americans were a match for the British.

Many Patriots acted heroically during the war.

**INTERACTIVE**

For extra help, review the 21st Century Tutorial: **Support Ideas With Evidence.**

# Practice Vocabulary

**True or False?** Decide whether each statement below is true or false.
Circle T or F, and then explain your answer. Be sure to include the
underlined vocabulary word or words in your explanation. The first one
is done for you.

1. **T / F** <u>Unalienable rights</u> are rights that cannot be claimed by citizens
   and can only be granted by governments.
   False; <u>Unalienable rights</u> are rights that *governments cannot take away*
   *from citizens.*

2. **T / F** A <u>traitor</u> is a person who fights for his or her country.

3. **T / F** King George III used <u>mercenaries</u> from Germany to help fight
   the colonists.

4. **T / F** The British used a <u>blockade</u> of colonial ports to help trade move
   smoothly between the colonies and Britain.

5. **T / F** The <u>preamble</u> of the Declaration of Independence declares that
   "all men are created equal."

6. **T / F** <u>Natural rights</u> are those that belong to all kings and queens
   from birth.

## Quick Activity  Edit the Declaration

Thomas Jefferson wrote the first draft of the Declaration of Independence in June 1776. Afterward, he made some revisions to the document himself, and Benjamin Franklin and John Adams also made some changes. When the Declaration was presented to the Second Continental Congress, still other changes were made.

Here is the original version of Thomas Jefferson's Preamble to the Declaration.

> We hold these truths to be sacred & undeniable; that all men are created equal & independent, that from that equal creation they derive rights inherent & inalienable, among which are the preservation of life, & liberty, & the pursuit of happiness. . . .

Working in pairs, one partner should write the original version of the Preamble on a piece of paper. The other should write any phrases from the final version of the Preamble (below) that differ from this original version on sticky notes. For example, you will have one sticky note that reads *self-evident*. Also use blank sticky notes to "cross out" words. Work together to use your sticky notes to change the original Preamble until it reads as the final version does.

> We hold these Truths to be self-evident, that all Men are created equal, that they are endowed by their Creator with certain unalienable Rights, that among these are Life, Liberty, and the Pursuit of Happiness.

**Team Challenge!** Work with your partner to answer this question: Why were these changes made to the Preamble? Give a possible reason for each change that was made.

# Take Notes

**Literacy Skills: Sequence** Use what you have read to complete the timeline. Look for key events that fall within the dates on the timeline as you read. Add those events to the timeline by entering the event in one of the spaces provided and then connecting the event to the appropriate place on the timeline. The first one has been completed for you.

**1778**
Molly Pitcher aids soldiers at Battle of Monmouth.

1778

1779

1780

1781

1782

1783

👆 **INTERACTIVE**

For extra help, review the 21st Century Tutorial: **Sequence**.

# Practice Vocabulary

**Matching Logic** Using your knowledge of the underlined vocabulary words, draw a line from each sentence in Column 1 to match it with the sentence in Column 2 to which it logically belongs.

| Column 1 | Column 2 |
| --- | --- |
| 1. More than 16,000 American and French troops laid <u>siege</u> to the general's army of fewer than 8,000. | The troops appeared suddenly out of the swamps, attacked quickly, and retreated swiftly back into the swamps. |
| 2. Congress <u>ratified</u> the Treaty of Paris after eight years of war. | Casimir Pulaski trained troops to fight from horseback. |
| 3. American forces included a <u>cavalry</u>. | Less than three weeks later, the British surrendered. |
| 4. Militia led by the Swamp Fox used <u>guerrilla</u> tactics against the British. | The British recognized the United States as an independent nation. |

# Writing Workshop Explanatory Essay

As you read, build a response to this question: **Why was there an American Revolution?** The prompts below will help walk you through the process.

### Lesson 1 Writing Task: Consider Your Purpose and Audience
(See Student Text, page 140)

Write a sentence that states the purpose of your essay and identifies your audience.

### Lesson 2 Writing Task: Develop a Clear Thesis (See Student Text, page 152)

In one sentence, express the most important reason for why the American Revolution happened. This will be your thesis statement for the explanatory essay you will write at the end of the topic.

### Lesson 3 Writing Task: Support Thesis with Details (See Student Text, page 163)

Now add details from lessons 1, 2, and 3 to support your thesis statement.

Lesson 1

Lesson 2

Lesson 3

## Lesson 4 Writing Task: Pick an Organizing Strategy

(See Student Text, page 176)

Make an outline of your essay. You can organize your essay any way you like. For example, you might focus first on British actions and then on changes in the colonial perspective. Or you might choose to organize by major themes, such as taxes. Use the chart below to decide on a strategy and outline how you will carry it out in each paragraph of your essay.

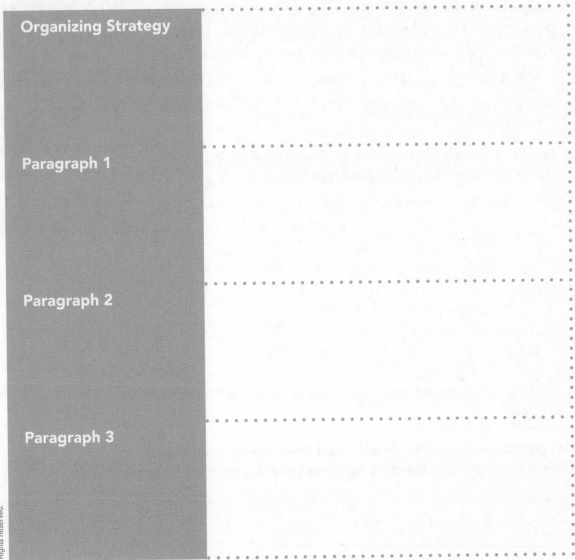

**Organizing Strategy**

**Paragraph 1**

**Paragraph 2**

**Paragraph 3**

## Lesson 5 Writing Task: Write an Introduction (See Student Text, page 188)

On a separate sheet of paper, write a short paragraph that introduces the thesis of your essay about the American Revolution.

### Writing Task (See Student Text, page 191)

Using the outline you created, answer the following question in a three-paragraph explanatory essay: Why was there an American Revolution?

# A Constitution for the United States Preview

## Essential Question How much power should the government have?

Before you begin this topic, think about the Essential Question by answering the following questions.

1. Read over the following list of powers. Put a check mark in front of each power that you think the government should have.

—declare war     —protect the environment     —build roads

—appoint a king     —tax the people     —fund schools

—censor newspapers     —spy on citizens     —make laws

2. For each item you did not check off, explain why you think the government should not have this power.

## Timeline Skills

As you read, write and/or draw at least three events from the topic. Draw a line from each event to its correct position on the timeline.

| 1770 | 1780 | 1790 |
| --- | --- | --- |

# Map Skills

Using maps throughout the topic, label the outline map with the places listed. Then shade the disputed western lands one color, Spanish territory a second color, and British territory a third color.

| | | | |
|---|---|---|---|
| Georgia | Delaware | Connecticut | Virginia |
| South Carolina | New Jersey | Rhode Island | New York |
| North Carolina | Pennsylvania | Massachusetts | New Hampshire |
| Maryland | | | |

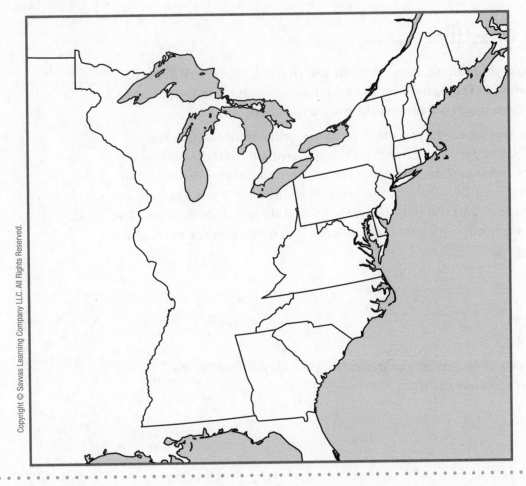

| 1800 | 1810 |
|---|---|

## Quest
Discussion Inquiry

# Senate Representation

On this Quest, you will explore sources and gather information about representation in the Senate from the perspective of a U.S. Senator. Then, you will participate in a civic discussion with other legislators about the Guiding Question.

### 1 Ask Questions (See Student Text, page 196)

As you begin your Quest, keep in mind the Guiding Question: **Should representation in the Senate be based on population?** and the Essential Question: **How much power should the government have?**

What other questions do you need to ask in order to answer these questions? Consider themes such as the government established by the Articles of Confederation, the concerns of the delegates who attended the Constitutional Convention, the ideas that influenced the Framers of the Constitution, and the debates within the states over ratification. Two questions are filled in for you. Add at least two questions for each of the other categories.

**Theme** The Articles of Confederation

Sample questions:

What was a major concern of the states when they agreed to the Articles of Confederation?

How was representation in Congress determined under the Articles?

**Theme** The Constitutional Convention

**Theme** Ideas and Traditions That Influenced the Framers

**Theme** Debates Over Ratification

**Theme** My Additional Questions

INTERACTIVE

For extra help with Step 1, review the
21st Century Tutorial: **Ask Questions**.

# Quest CONNECTIONS

## ② Investigate

As you read about the events leading up to and following the drafting of the Constitution, collect five connections from your text to help you answer the Guiding Question. Three connections are already chosen for you.

## Connect to Alexander Hamilton

**Primary Source** Federalist and Antifederalist Writings
(See Student Text, page 223)

Here's a connection! Read the excerpt from Framer Alexander Hamilton. To what criticism of the proposed Constitution is he responding?

According to Hamilton, what is accomplished by equal representation in the Senate?

## Connect to The Virginia and New Jersey Plans

**Lesson 2** Disagreements Over a New Government (See Student Text, page 206)

Here's another connection! Read the discussion of the Virginia and New Jersey plans in your text. What was the main difference between the two plans?

How did the states respond to these two plans?

## Connect to Representation in Congress

**Lesson 5** The Legislative Branch—Congress (See Student Text, page 229)

What does this connection tell you about how the number of representatives is decided in each body that makes up the legislative branch? How many representatives does each state get in the House? How many representatives does each state get in the Senate?

Which states have the largest and smallest numbers of representatives?

It's Your Turn! **Find two more connections. Fill in the title of your connections, then answer the questions. Connections may be images, primary sources, maps, or text.**

## Your Choice | Connect to

### Location in text

What is the main idea of this connection?

What does it tell you about how representation in the Senate should be determined?

## Your Choice | Connect to

### Location in text

What is the main idea of this connection?

What does it tell you about how representation in the Senate should be determined?

**3** **Examine Primary Sources** (See Student Text, page 254)

Examine the primary and secondary sources provided online or from your teacher. Fill in the chart to show how these sources provide further information about whether representation in the Senate should be based on population. The first one is completed for you.

| Should Representation in the Senate be Based on Population? | |
| --- | --- |
| Source | Yes or No? Why? |
| "Democracy-Proof" | YES, because equal representation unfairly allows a small minority to pass or block laws. |
| "Democracy's False Prophet" | |
| "America the Undemocratic?" | |

**INTERACTIVE**

For extra help with Step 3, review the 21st Century Tutorials: **Compare viewpoints** and **Read Charts, Graphs, and Tables**.

## 4 Discuss! (See Student Text, page 254)

Now that you have collected clues and explored documents about representation in Congress, you are ready to discuss with your fellow representatives the Guiding Question: **Should representation in the Senate be based on population?** Follow the steps below, using the spaces provided to prepare for your discussion.

You will work with a partner in a small group of Senators. Try to reach consensus, a situation in which everyone is in agreement, on the question. The people of your state are depending on you!

1. **Prepare Your Arguments** You will be assigned a position on the question, either YES or NO.

My position: ...............................................................

Work with your partner to review your Quest notes from the Quest Connections and Quest Sources.

- If you were assigned YES, agree with your partner on what you think were the strongest arguments from Scialabba.

- If you were assigned NO, agree on what you think were the strongest arguments from Gordon and Zakaria.

2. **Present Your Position** Those assigned YES will present their arguments and evidence first. As you listen, ask clarifying questions to gain information and understanding.

---

### What is a Clarifying Question?

These types of questions do not judge the person talking. They are only for the listener to be clear on what he or she is hearing.

| Example: | Example: |
| --- | --- |
| Can you tell me more about that? | You said [x]. Am I getting that right? |

---

**INTERACTIVE**

For extra help with Step 4, review the 21st Century Tutorial: **Participate in a Discussion or Debate**.

# Practice Vocabulary

**Vocabulary Quiz Show** Some quiz shows ask a question and expect the contestant to give the answer. In other shows, the contestant is given an answer and must supply the question. If the blank is in the Question column, write the question that would result in the answer in the Answer column. If the question is supplied, write the answer.

## Question

1.

2. Under which plan was the number of representatives based on population?

3.

4.

5. What is the name of the compromise that solved the issue of representation in Congress?

6.

## Answer

1. Constitutional Convention

2.

3. New Jersey Plan

4. compromise

5.

6. Three-Fifths Compromise

## Quick Activity  Focus on a Framer

With a partner or small group, examine this short biography of framer James Madison.

**Did you know?**

Often sleeping only four hours a night, James Madison graduated from the College of New Jersey (today, Princeton University) in just two years.

James Madison Jr. was the eldest of ten children. He grew up at Montpelier, a 5,000-acre plantation in Virginia. Frequently ill and painfully shy, at 12 he began studying Greek, Latin, French, geography, mathematics, and literature. Later he attended the College of New Jersey at Princeton. In 1776, Madison was elected to the Virginia Constitutional Convention, where he impressed members with his grasp of political philosophy. He next served in the Continental Congress, and then the state legislature. During this time, Madison spent long hours poring over books of history, government, and law. In 1787, he traveled to Philadelphia as one of Virginia's delegates to the Constitutional Convention. Many years later, he served as the fourth President of the United States.

James Madison's father was a leading landowner in Virginia. What are two other key features of James Madison's background?

The excerpt below is taken from the notes James Madison took during the Constitutional Convention. In it, he is arguing against the New Jersey Plan.

[James Madison] enumerated [listed] the objections against an equality of votes in the second branch. . . . 1. The minority could [negate] the will of the majority of the people. 2. They could extort [get by force] measures, by making them a condition of their assent [agreement] to other necessary measures. 3. They could obtrude [force] measures on the majority, by virtue of the peculiar powers which would be vested in the Senate. 4. The evil, instead of being cured by time, would increase with every new State that should be admitted, as they must all be admitted on the principle of equality.

— James Madison, *Debates in the Federal Convention of 1787, July 14, 1787*

**Team Challenge!**  What point is James Madison making in this excerpt? Work together to draw conclusions about the relationship between Madison's background and the point of view he expresses in the excerpt. Write a short paragraph explaining your conclusions.

# Take Notes

**Literacy Skills: Classify and Categorize** Use what you have read to complete the table. Write the most important ideas from each group that influenced the founders as they wrote the Constitution. The first one has been completed for you.

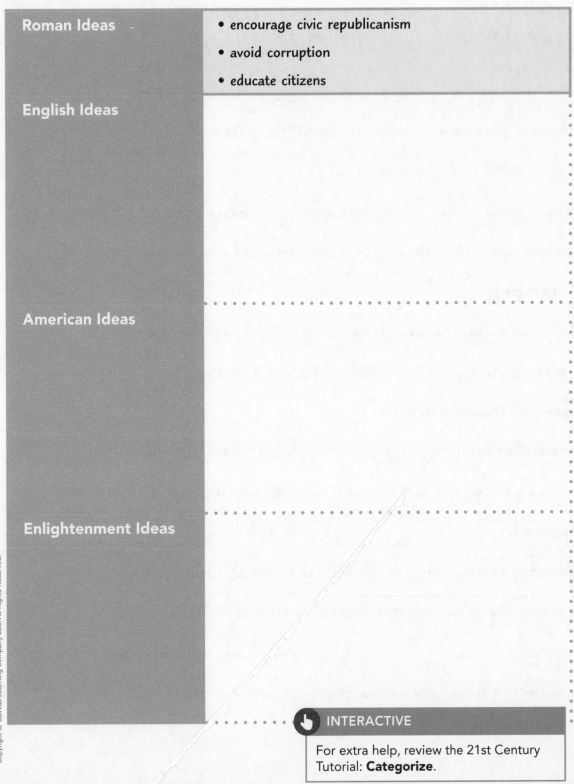

| Roman Ideas | • encourage civic republicanism<br>• avoid corruption<br>• educate citizens |
|---|---|
| **English Ideas** | |
| **American Ideas** | |
| **Enlightenment Ideas** | |

**INTERACTIVE**

For extra help, review the 21st Century Tutorial: **Categorize**.

## Practice Vocabulary

**Use a Word Bank** Choose one word from the word bank to fill in each blank. When you have finished, you will have a short summary of important ideas from the section.

### Word Bank

| | | |
|---|---|---|
| republic | dictatorship | Magna Carta |
| English Bill of Rights | separation of powers | |

The Framers of the Constitution drew on many ideas as they worked

to create a new government for the United States. They looked to

ancient Rome, for example, which was a ......................... ,

a government in which citizens rule themselves through elected

representatives. They also considered the ideas put forward in great

English documents. The .......................... stated that

kings had to obey the law and that the nobles had certain rights. Other

important ideas, such as the right to trial by jury, were found in a

document created in 1689, the ......................... .

In addition to protecting the rights of the people, the Framers also

knew it was important to make sure the new government would not

become a ......................... , a government in which one

person or a small group of people holds all the power. To prevent this

from happening, they included important principles in the Constitution,

such as the ......................... , which says that the powers

of government should be divided up among several branches.

## Take Notes

**Literacy Skills: Sequence** Use what you have read to complete the timeline. Determine the date for each of the events listed. Then, draw a line from each event to its correct position on the timeline.

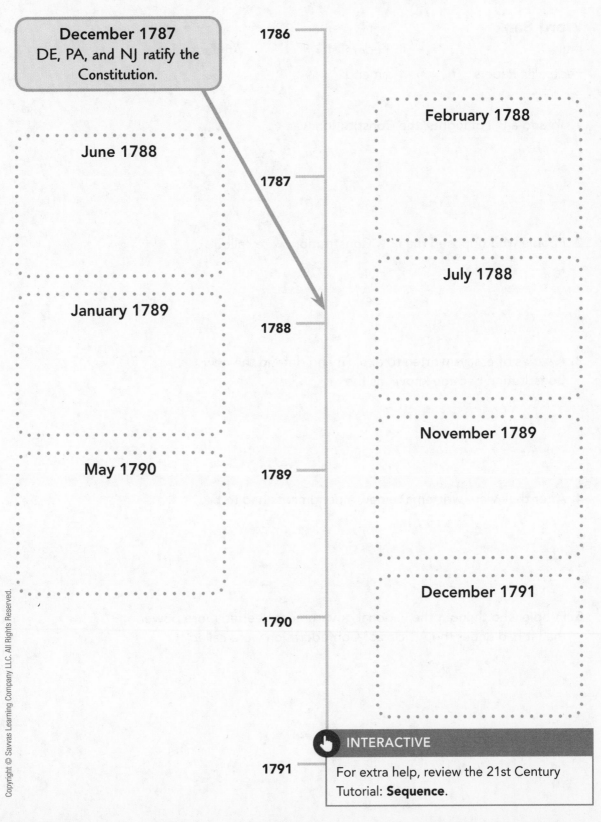

**December 1787**
DE, PA, and NJ ratify the Constitution.

1786

1787

**February 1788**

**June 1788**

**July 1788**

1788

**January 1789**

**November 1789**

**May 1790**

1789

**December 1791**

1790

INTERACTIVE

1791

For extra help, review the 21st Century Tutorial: **Sequence**.

## Practice Vocabulary

**Sentence Builder** Finish the sentences below with a key term from the Word Bank. You may have to change the form of the words to complete the sentences.

### Word Bank

| | | |
|---|---|---|
| ratify | Federalist | Antifederalist |
| Federalist Papers | amend | |

1. To add a Bill of Rights, the Constitution was

2. People who opposed the new Constitution were called

3. A series of essays written to explain and defend the new Constitution became known as the

4. After they were written, the new amendments had to be

5. People who thought the national government needed more power than it had under the Articles of Confederation were called

## Take Notes

**Literacy Skills: Classify and Categorize** Use what you have read to complete the table. Place each key term under its proper category. The first one has been completed for you.

### Key Terms

Preamble

27 amendments

Preamble

Popular sovereignty

Executive

Vice President and executive
  departments

Checks and balances

Judicial

Federalism

Seven articles

President

District courts

Limited government

Legislative

Separation of powers

House of Representatives

Individual rights

Republicanism

Supreme Court

Senate

| Basic Principles | Constitution | Government Structure |
|---|---|---|
| | Preamble | |

**INTERACTIVE**

For extra help, review the 21st Century Tutorial: **Categorize**.

# Practice Vocabulary

**Word Map** Study the word map for the word *veto*. Characteristics are words or phrases that relate to the word in the center of the word map. Non-characteristics are words and phrases not associated with the word. Use the blank word map to explore the meaning of the word *bill*. Then make word maps of your own for these words: *popular sovereignty*, *override*, and *impeach*.

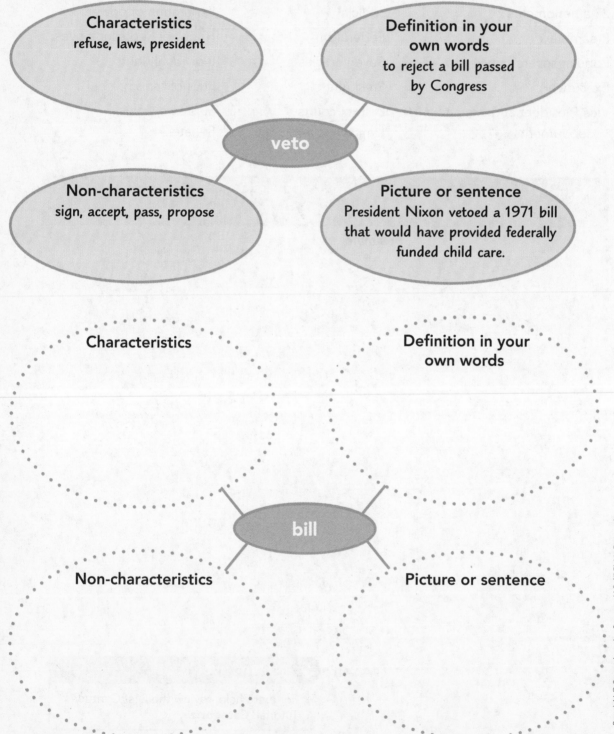

**Characteristics**
refuse, laws, president

**Definition in your own words**
to reject a bill passed by Congress

**veto**

**Non-characteristics**
sign, accept, pass, propose

**Picture or sentence**
President Nixon vetoed a 1971 bill that would have provided federally funded child care.

**Characteristics**

**Definition in your own words**

**bill**

**Non-characteristics**

**Picture or sentence**

## Take Notes

**Literacy Skills: Summarize** Use what you have read to complete the chart. List the most important points from each section of the text in the lower boxes. Then summarize the entire lesson in the top box. The first section has been completed for you.

**Summary:**

### Amendment Methods

1. There are two methods for proposing amendments and two methods for ratifying amendments.

2. All amendments were proposed using the same method.

3. All but the 21st Amendment were ratified in the same way.

### The Amendments

1.

2.

3.

### State Government

1.

2.

3.

### Local Government

1.

2.

3.

👆 **INTERACTIVE**

For extra help, review the 21st Century Tutorial: **Summarize**.

# Practice Vocabulary

**Words in Context** For each question below, write an answer that shows your understanding of the boldfaced key term.

1. What is the **Bill of Rights**, and why is it important to all Americans?

2. What is the opposite of a **civil** trial?

3. What is a **constitutional initiative** and how is it an example of democracy at work?

4. What is meant by a state's **infrastructure**?

5. What is **local government** and in what major way does it differ from the state and national governments?

# Quick Activity  Explore Free Speech

With a partner or small group, examine this cartoon related to the Bill of Rights. It was created when George W. Bush was president.

To which amendment from the Bill of Rights does this cartoon relate? What point is the artist making with the signs in people's yards? Why does the man walking down the street say "America the Beautiful"?

## Did you know?

Not all countries allow freedom of speech. North Korea, Cuba, Libya, and others restrict the use of the Internet and do not allow citizens to criticize the government.

**Team Challenge!** Are there ever times when speech should not be protected? Consider the situations below and discuss with your group whether or not each should be allowed. Put a check mark beside the examples of speech you think should be protected.

___blog that criticizes a member of Congress

___book that gives information that endangers national security

___ad that falsely claims a product will make you smarter

___speech that urges protestors to attack the police

___editorial that accuses a governor of stealing money

___burning a cross in someone's front yard

___protestors chanting in front of the White House

___network news story exposing wrongdoing by the president

# Take Notes

**Literacy Skills: Use Evidence to Support Ideas** Use what you have read to complete the chart. Use the evidence in the lower boxes to arrive at a conclusion. Write your conclusion in the top box.

Conclusion:

At least one parent is a U.S. citizen.

You were naturalized.

You were 18 or younger when your parents were naturalized.

Conclusion:

Citizens have a duty to obey the laws.

Citizens have a duty to help defend the nation.

Citizens have a duty to serve on juries.

**INTERACTIVE**

For extra help, review the 21st Century Tutorial: **Support Ideas with Evidence**.

# Practice Vocabulary

**Sentence Revision** Revise each sentence so that the underlined vocabulary word is used logically. Be sure not to change the vocabulary word. The first one is done for you.

1. A <u>citizen</u> is a person who owes loyalty to no particular nation and is entitled to no rights or protections.

   A <u>citizen</u> is a person who owes loyalty to a particular nation and is entitled to all its rights and protections.

2. If you have not yet completed the official legal process for becoming a citizen, you are a <u>naturalized</u> citizen.

3. An <u>immigrant</u> is a person who leaves a country in order to return to his or her country of birth.

4. An immigrant must receive permission to remain in the United States as a <u>resident alien</u>, or citizen living out of the country.

5. <u>Civic virtue</u> is the willingness of the government to grant all American citizens equal rights under the law.

6. <u>Patriotism</u> is a feeling of love and devotion toward other countries.

7. Every citizen has the responsibility to report for <u>jury duty</u>, meaning to decide whether a jury reached the correct decision.

# Writing Workshop Arguments

As you read, build a response to this question: **How much power should the federal government have, and what should its responsibilities be?** The prompts below will help walk you through the process.

### Lesson 1 Writing Task: Introduce Claims (See Student Text, page 203)

Write a brief paragraph introducing the two sides of the argument about how much power the government should have.

### Lessons 2 and 3 Writing Tasks: Support Claims and Distinguish Claims from Opposing Claims (See Student Text, pages 209 and 215)

Based on the information in Lessons 1, 2, and 3, write a few sentences that support each claim about how much power the government should have. Then, for each claim, write a counterclaim. Be sure to use logical reasoning and support your position with evidence.

|  | Supporting Details | Counterclaim |
|---|---|---|
| Claim 1 |  |  |
| Claim 2 |  |  |

**Lesson 4 Writing Task: Use Credible Sources** (See Student Text, page 222)

On additional paper, make a list of sources you might use to support or oppose claims about how much power the federal government should have.

**Lessons 5 and 6 Writing Tasks: Use Transition Words and Shape Tone**
(See Student Text, pages 236 and 245)

Transition words and phrases can help compare ideas (*similarly*), contrast them (*but, on the contrary*), or clarify them (*to put it another way*). Think of more transition words and phrases and write them here. Then, think about the tone you want to take in your argument. To help shape your tone, write a few sentences that reflect your viewpoint about the subject matter, while maintaining the formal style and informative approach required in presenting an argument.

**Transition Words**

**Tone**

**Lesson 7 Writing Task: Write a Conclusion** (See Student Text, page 252)

Now that you have formed your own viewpoint about how much power the government should have, write a conclusion for your argument.

**Writing Task** (See Student Text, page 252)

Using the claims, evidence, and sources you have listed here, answer the following question in a three-paragraph argument: How much power should the federal government have, and what should its responsibilities be?

## Essential Question How much power should the federal government have, and what should it do?

Before you begin this topic, think about the Essential Question by completing the following activity.

1. Write a short blog post that explains how much power the federal government should have, and why.

## Timeline Skills

As you read, write and/or draw at least three events from the topic. Draw a line from each event to its correct position on the timeline.

| 1780 | 1790 | 1800 |
|------|------|------|

# Map Skills

Using maps throughout the topic, label the outline map with the places listed. Then color in the bodies of water.

Louisiana Purchase

land from Great Britain 1783

thirteen states in 1783

land from Spain 1819

Great Lakes

land from Great Britain 1818

Mississippi River

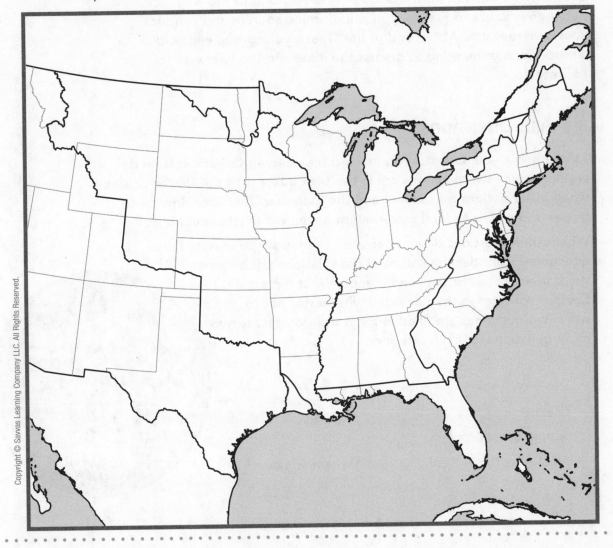

| 1810 | 1820 | 1830 | 1840 |
|------|------|------|------|

## Quest
### Project-Based Learning Inquiry

# Stay Out? Or Get Involved?

On this Quest, you are working as a member of President Jefferson's Cabinet. The Cabinet must decide how to respond to the war between Britain and France. You will examine sources and conduct your own research. At the end of the Quest, your group will hold a mock Cabinet meeting to discuss the issue and the best way to address it.

### 1 Ask Questions (See Student Text, page 260)

As you begin your Quest, keep in mind the Guiding Question: **How do we determine which actions are in the best interest of the United States when other nations go to war?** and the Essential Question: **How much power should the federal government have, and what should it do?**

What other questions do you need to ask in order to answer these questions? Consider the nature of the relationships between the United States, Britain, and France. What factors did the Cabinet consider as they debated whether or not to go to war? Two questions are filled in for you. Add at least two more questions for each category.

**Theme** Political

Sample questions:

What were the political objectives of the new nation?

Did the United States still have obligations to its ally France?

**Theme** Economic

**Theme** Relations with Other Countries

**Theme** My Additional Questions

INTERACTIVE

For extra help with Step 1, review the
21st Century Tutorial: **Ask Questions**.

# Quest CONNECTIONS

## 2 Investigate

As you read about the Early Republic, collect five connections to help you answer the Guiding Question. Three connections are already chosen for you.

## Connect to President Washington's Foreign Policy

**Lesson 1  How Did Americans React to the French Revolution?**
(See Student Text, page 270)

Here's a connection! Read this section in your text. What does it tell you about how the United States reacted to the war in Europe? Why did the President choose this course of action? What did it establish?

How did President Washington enforce his policy?

## Connect to the XYZ Affair

**Lesson 3** Conflict With France (See Student Text, page 282)

Here's another connection! Read this section in your text. Think about the XYZ Affair and the way that President Adams responded to French attacks on American ships. What do these events suggest about dealing with conflicts?

How did Americans respond to these events?

## Connect to American Embargo

**Lesson 4** A Ban on Trade (See Student Text, page 301)

What does this connection tell you about the pros and cons of President Jefferson's ban on trade?

Could Jefferson's actions have started a war?

It's Your Turn! **Find two more connections. Fill in the title of your connections, then answer the questions. Connections may be images, primary sources, maps, or text.**

## Your Choice | Connect to

### Location in text

What is the main idea of this connection?

What does it tell you about how the United States reacted to war in other nations? What does it tell you about how the United States established its foreign policy?

## Your Choice | Connect to

### Location in text

What is the main idea of this connection?

What does it tell you about how the United States reacted to the war in other nations? What does it tell you about how the United States established its foreign policy?

## ③ Conduct Research (See Student Text, page 330)

Explore primary and secondary sources about events leading up to 1793, when war broke out between Britain and France. Fill in the chart to show how these sources provide further information about how we determine which actions are in the best interest of the United States when other nations go to war. The first entry is completed for you.

| Source | How do we determine which actions are in the best interest of the United States when other nations go to war? |
|---|---|
| Washington's Farewell Address | Maintaining a policy of neutrality is the best policy for the nation at this time. |
| | |
| | |
| | |

👆 **INTERACTIVE**

For extra help with Step 3, review the 21st Century Tutorial: **Analyze Primary and Secondary Sources**.

## 4 Write a Position Paper (See Student Text, page 330)

Now it is time to put together all of the information you have gathered and use it to hold a mock Cabinet meeting with your team to review notes, decide on the best course of action, and document this problem-solving process. In a small group, write a position paper summarizing the chosen solution.

1. **Prepare to Write**  You have collected connections and explored primary and secondary sources about how the United States regarded the affairs of other nations. Look through your notes and decide which events and statements you want to highlight in your position paper. Record them here.

### Events and Statements

2. **Write a Draft** Using evidence from the text and the documents you explored, write a draft of the position paper based on the outcome of the mock Cabinet meeting.

3. **Share with a Partner** Exchange your draft with a partner. Tell your partner what you like about his or her draft and suggest any improvements you think are necessary.

4. **Finalize Your Paper** Revise your position paper as needed. Correct any grammatical or spelling errors.

5. **Reflect on the Quest** Think about your experience completing this topic's Quest. What did you learn about the United States and its position on foreign affairs in the early days of the Republic? Do you still have questions about the position of the United States on foreign events at that time? How will you answer them?

**Reflections**

 **INTERACTIVE**

For extra help, review the 21st Century Tutorials: **Work in Teams** and **Make Decisions**.

# Take Notes

**Literacy Skills: Summarize** Use what you have read to complete the chart. Add details related to the challenges facing the new government in each box. The first entry has been completed for you.

**Challenges Facing the New Government**

## The Government

- In 1789, Congress creates the departments of State, Treasury, and War and the offices of Attorney General and Postmaster General.
- Washington sets a precedent by choosing well-known leaders to serve in his Cabinet—Thomas Jefferson and Alexander Hamilton.
- Congress passes the Judiciary Act of 1789 establishing the Supreme Court.

## The Economy

## Foreign Affairs

**INTERACTIVE**

For extra help, review the 21st Century Tutorial: **Summarize**.

# Practice Vocabulary

**Matching Logic** Using your knowledge of the underlined vocabulary words, draw a line from each sentence in Column 1 to match it with a sentence in Column 2 to which it logically belongs.

| Column 1 | Column 2 |
|----------|----------|
| In his first major task as President, Washington chose talented people to fill his <u>Cabinet</u>. | James Madison did not approve of investors making a profit in this way. |
| Washington's presidency, being the first, established <u>precedents</u> that are still used today. | In 1789, Congress passed this tax on imported goods to protect their products. |
| On April 30, at Federal Hall, the <u>inauguration</u> of George Washington took place. | The number of executive departments has more than tripled. There are now fourteen executive departments. |
| Faced with the conflict between France and Britain, President Washington chose to remain <u>neutral</u>. | Hamilton's plan proposed using these to promise payment to citizens. |
| To help pay off war debts, the government issued <u>bonds</u> with a promise to repay the loans with interest. | In 1796, he decided not to run for a third term. Not until 1940 did any President seek a third term. |
| Hamilton believed a <u>tariff</u> would help with the new government's debt. | Britain made matters difficult for the United States when it seized cargo from American ships. |
| <u>Speculators</u> bought war bonds in the hopes of making a profit. | This ceremony starts a new presidency. |

# Take Notes

**Literacy Skills: Compare and Contrast** Use what you have read to complete the table. Compare and contrast the political views of the first political parties. The first entry is completed for you.

| The First Political Parties | |
| --- | --- |
| **Federalists** | **Democratic-Republicans** |
| strong national government | limited national government |
|  |  |
|  |  |
|  |  |
|  |  |
|  |  |

**INTERACTIVE**

For extra help, review the 21st Century Tutorial: **Compare and Contrast**.

# Practice Vocabulary

**True or False?** Decide whether each statement below is true or false. Circle T or F, and then explain your answer. Be sure to include the underlined word in your explanation. The first one is done for you.

1. **T / F** The legislative branch has the final word on whether or not a law is <u>unconstitutional</u>.
   False; The Supreme Court has the final word on whether or not a law is <u>unconstitutional</u>.

2. **T / F** The <u>Federalists</u> gained wide support from farmers, southern planters, and workers.

3. **T / F** Differing views on what the nation should become led to <u>factions</u> and the rise of political parties.

4. **T / F** <u>Democratic Republicans</u> favored a loose interpretation of the Constitution.

## Quick Activity  Take Sides

Look at the political cartoon. Clearly, despite President Washington's warning against political parties, Americans were deeply divided over how the nation should be run.

With a partner or small group, discuss the issues over which Democratic Republicans and Federalists disagreed. Decide whether you would support Hamilton's or Jefferson's views on the role of government.

Team Challenge!  Still working with a partner or small group, list what you consider to be the strengths and weaknesses of having political parties in a nation. Use this list to write a three or four sentence paragraph explaining why you favor or oppose having political parties.

| Strengths | Weaknesses |
| --- | --- |
|  |  |

# Take Notes

**Literacy Skills: Identify Main Ideas** Use what you have read to complete the concept webs. In the first concept web, list the main idea and details of the foreign policy issues John Adams faced during his presidency. The first entry is completed for you. In the second concept web, list the changes Jefferson made to the government during his presidency.

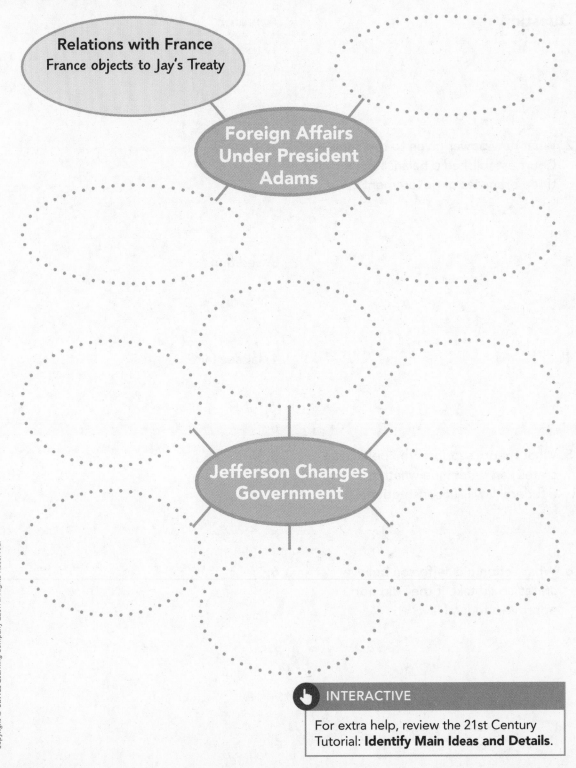

**Relations with France**
France objects to Jay's Treaty

Foreign Affairs Under President Adams

Jefferson Changes Government

🖑 INTERACTIVE

For extra help, review the 21st Century Tutorial: **Identify Main Ideas and Details.**

# Practice Vocabulary

**Vocabulary Quiz Show** Some quiz shows ask a question and expect the contestant to give the answer. In other shows, the contestant is given an answer and must supply the question. If the blank is in the Question column, write the question that would result in the answer in the Answer column. If the question is supplied, write the answer.

| Question | Answer |
| --- | --- |
| 1. | 1. tribute |
| 2. What new power given to the Supreme Court established a balance among the three branches of government? | 2. |
| 3. | 3. sedition |
| 4. | 4. laissez faire |
| 5. What theory supports the belief that states can determine whether or not a federal law is unconstitutional? | 5. |
| 6. What action did Jefferson believe states could take if they did not approve a federal law? | 6. |

## Quick Activity Explore

President Jefferson instructed Lewis and Clark to explore a possible overland route to the Pacific and determine if the Missouri River offered "the most direct and practicable water communication across [the] continent." Jefferson was also interested in the port city of New Orleans, which was a part of the Louisiana Purchase.

With a partner or a small group, discuss why the President insisted on these goals as part of the expedition. Why were rivers so important?

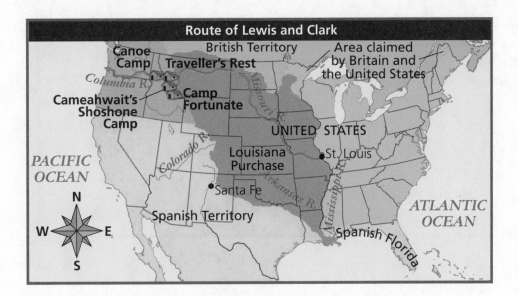

Team Challenge! With your partner or group, write an entry that a member of the Lewis and Clark expedition might have written in their journal years after their expedition to describe how rivers changed life in the United States. Share your journal entry with the class.

## Take Notes

**Literacy Skills: Sequence** Use what you have read to complete the flowchart. Provide the sequence of events that led to the War of 1812. The first entry is completed for you.

Relations with Great Britain were strained. Britain provided weapons and support to American Indians who attacked American settlers in the West.

INTERACTIVE

For extra help, review the 21st Century Tutorial: **Sequence**.

# Practice Vocabulary

**Word Map** Study the word map for the word *nationalism*. Characteristics are words or phrases that relate to the word in the center of the word map. Non-characteristics are words and phrases not associated with the word. Use the blank word map to explore the meaning of the term *War Hawks*. Then make word maps of your own for the word *confederation*.

**Characteristics**
common bond, unity, patriotic pride

**Definition in your own words**
a feeling of pride, loyalty, and protectiveness toward one's country

**nationalism**

**Non-characteristics**
divided, anger

**Picture or sentence**
The War of 1812 sent strong feelings of nationalism throughout the nation.

**Characteristics**

**Definition in your own words**

**War Hawks**

**Non-Characteristics**

**Picture or sentence**

# Take Notes

**Literacy Skills: Draw Conclusions** Use what you have read to draw conclusions about the effect of several Supreme Court decisions on the way the government was run. Complete the flowchart outlining the cases and the decisions. In the bottom box, write one or two sentences about how these Supreme Court decisions affected the U.S. government. The first one has been started for you.

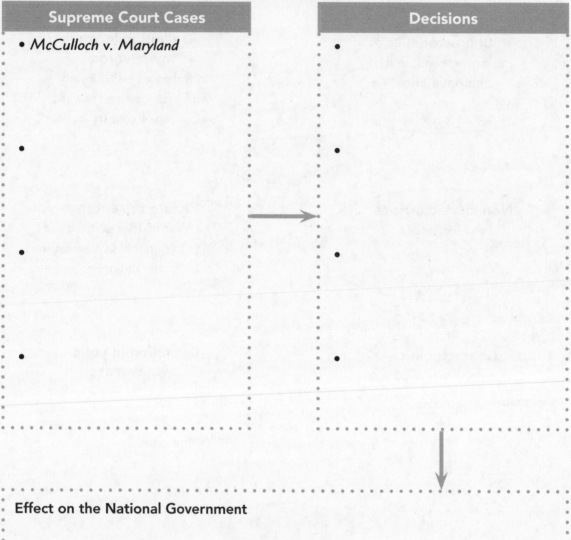

| Supreme Court Cases | Decisions |
| --- | --- |
| • McCulloch v. Maryland | • |
| • | • |
| • | • |
| • | • |

**Effect on the National Government**

**INTERACTIVE**

For extra help, review the 21st Century Tutorial: **Draw Conclusions**.

# Practice Vocabulary

**Use a Word Bank** Choose one word from the word bank to fill in each blank. When you have finished, you will have a short summary of important ideas from the section.

## Word Bank

sectionalism

interstate commerce

intervention

American System

Monroe Doctrine

Nationalism sparked President Monroe's presentation of a plan to improve the economy of the nation. The three-part plan, designed by Henry Clay, was called the ............................... . The plan would unify the economy of the states into a national economy. During the Monroe administration, several landmark Supreme Court decisions promoted national unity by strengthening the federal government. One decision, *Gibbons* v. *Ogden*, stated that ............................... could be regulated only by the federal government. At the same time nationalism was uniting the country, loyalty to one's region or ............................... was threatening to drive the country apart. The economy, slavery, and states' rights were major issues.

Events elsewhere in the Americas loomed large. Presenting the United States as a world power and protector of Latin America, the ............................... firmly stated that European ............................... would not be tolerated.

# Writing Workshop Research Paper

As you read, build a response to this prompt: **Research the country's physical landscapes, political divisions, and territorial expansion during the early republic.** The prompts below will help you walk through the process.

## Lesson 1 Writing Task: Generate Questions to Focus Research
(See Student Text, page 272)

At the end of this topic, you will write a research paper describing the country's physical geography, political divisions, and expansion during the terms of its first four Presidents. Make a list of questions that would need to be answered in order to write a research paper on this subject, such as: What were the political parties of this period?

## Lesson 2 Writing Task: Find and Use Credible Sources
(See Student Text, page 279)

You will need more information to write your paper. List three credible sources of information you can use to research about the early republic's physical landscapes, political divisions, or territorial expansion.

## Lesson 3 Writing Tasks: Choose an Organizing Strategy
(See Student Text, page 290)

How will you organize your research paper? Will you have one section for each topic? Chronologically? Choose an organizing strategy for your paper and describe it here.

**Lesson 4 Writing Task: Support Thesis with Details** (See Student Text, page 302)

Gather specific details from each lesson that you can use in your research paper. Write those details in the table below.

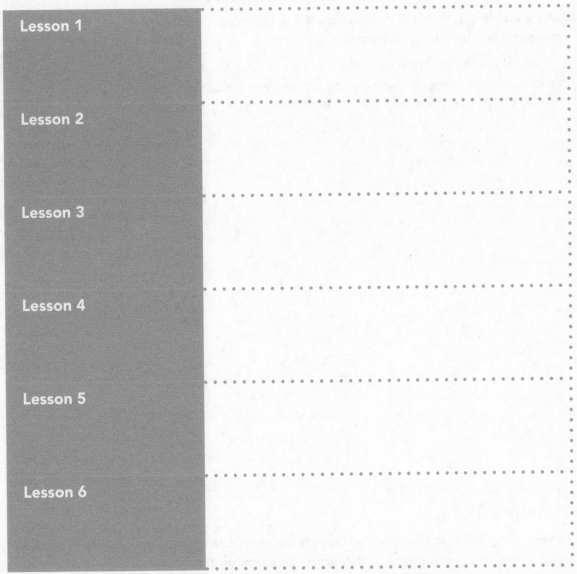

| Lesson 1 | |
| --- | --- |
| Lesson 2 | |
| Lesson 3 | |
| Lesson 4 | |
| Lesson 5 | |
| Lesson 6 | |

**Lesson 5 Writing Task: Clarify Relationships with Transition Words**
(See Student Text, page 315)

What are some transition words that you can use to show the relationship between facts in your paper? Write those words on a separate sheet of paper.

**Lesson 6 Writing Task: Visuals** (See Student Text, page 328)

What graphics and formatting will you use to help convey information in an engaging way? Make a list on a separate sheet of paper.

**Writing Task** (See Student Text, page 331)

Using your notes, write a research paper describing the country's physical geography, political divisions, and expansion during the terms of the first four Presidents.

# 6 The Age of Jackson and Westward Expansion Preview

## Essential Question Why do people move?

Before you begin this topic, think about the Essential Question by answering the following questions.

1. If you had the option to move to any city or country in the world, where would you choose to go and why? Include at least three reasons why you chose that location.

## Timeline Skills

As you read, write and/or draw at least three events from the topic. Draw a line from each event to its correct position on the timeline.

| 1820 | 1830 |
|------|------|

# Map Skills

Using maps throughout the topic, label the outline map with the places listed. Then, color in the bodies of water.

Gadsen Purchase

Pacific Ocean

Texas Annexation

Land ceded by Britain in 1818

Louisiana Purchase

Oregon Country

Mexico

Gulf of Mexico

1840

1850

1860

## Quest
### Civic Discussion Inquiry

# The Mexican-American War

On this Quest, you will explore sources and gather information about the Mexican-American War in the role of a modern historian. Then, you will participate in a civic discussion with other historians about the Guiding Question.

## 1 Ask Questions (See Student Text, page 336)

As you begin your Quest, keep in mind the Guiding Question: **Was the Mexican-American War justified?** and the Essential Question: **Why do people move?**

What other questions do you need to ask in order to answer these questions? Consider that the dispute between the United States and Mexico over the boundary of the southern border of Texas remained hostile. Two questions are filled in for you. Add at least two questions for each category.

**Theme** Troubles with Mexico

Sample questions:

What were the hostilities about?

What was President Polk's view?

**Theme** Manifest Destiny and Westward Expansion

**Theme** Public Response to the War

**Theme** Effects of the War

**Theme** My Additional Questions

 INTERACTIVE

For additional help with Step 1, review the 21st Century Tutorial: **Ask Questions**.

# Quest CONNECTIONS

## 2 Investigate

As you read about the Mexican-American War, collect five connections to help you answer the Guiding Question. Three connections are already chosen for you.

## Connect to Colonies in Texas

**Lesson 6** Americans Colonize Mexican Texas (See Student Text, page 386)

Here's a connection! Read this section in your text. What does this event tell you about the significance of Texas and Mexico to the United States?

How did the United States' relationship with Mexico develop after Mexican independence from Spain?

## Connect to Causes of the Mexican-American War

**Lesson 7**  The Mexican-American War (See Student Text, page 394)

Here's another connection! Read this section in your text.
What events led to the start of the war with Mexico?

How did most Americans feel about the war?

## Connect to Effects of the Mexican-American War

**Lesson 7**  Mormons Settle the Mexican Cession (See Student Text, page 397)

What does this connection tell you about the immediate effect of the war's end?

What were the long-term effects of the war for the United States?

It's Your Turn!  **Find two more connections. Fill in the title of your connections. Then, answer the questions. Connections may be images, primary sources, maps, or text.**

## Your Choice | Connect to

### Location in text

What is the main idea of this connection?

What does it tell you about the relationship between the United States and Mexico?

## Your Choice | Connect to

### Location in text

What is the main idea of this connection?

What does it tell you about the relationship between the United States and Mexico?

# 3 Examine Primary Sources (See Student Text, page 402)

Examine the primary and secondary sources provided online or from your teacher. Fill in the chart to show how these sources provide further information about whether the Mexican-American War was justified. The first one is completed for you.

| Was the Mexican-American War Justified? | |
|---|---|
| **Source** | **Yes or No? Why?** |
| *"The Borderlands on the Eve of War"* | YES. Events in Mexico had weakened the government, revolts were breaking out, there was political chaos and a poor economy. In addition, Mexicans no longer felt a sense of loyalty to the government. |
| **Message on War with Mexico** | |
| **The War with Mexico** | |
| *The History of Mexico* | |

👆 INTERACTIVE

For extra help with Step 3, review the 21st Century Tutorials: **Compare Viewpoints** and **Read Charts, Graphs, and Tables**.

## Quest FINDINGS

### 4 Discuss! (See Student Text, page 402)

Now that you have collected evidence and explored primary and secondary sources about the Mexican-American War, you are ready to discuss with your fellow historians the Guiding Question: **Was the Mexican-American War justified?**

You will work with a partner in a small group of historians. Try to reach a consensus, or a situation in which everyone is in agreement, on the question. Can you do it?

1. **Prepare Your Arguments** You will be assigned a position on the question, either YES or NO.

My position: :.................................................:

Work with your partner to review your Quest notes from the Quest Connections and Quest Sources.

- If you were assigned YES, agree with your partner on what you think were the strongest arguments from Weber and Polk.

- If you were assigned NO, agree on what you think were the strongest arguments from Lincoln and Corkwood.

2. **Present Your Position** Those assigned YES will present their arguments and evidence first. As you listen to the opposing side, ask clarifying questions to gain information and understanding.

| What is a Clarifying Question? | |
|---|---|
| These types of questions do not judge the person talking. They are only for the listener to be clear on what he or she is hearing. | |
| Examples:<br>Can you tell me more about that? | Examples:<br>You said [x]. Am I getting that right? |

**INTERACTIVE**

For extra help with Step 4, review the 21st Century Tutorial: **Participate in a Discussion or Debate.**

While the opposite side speaks, take notes on what you hear in the space below.

3. **Switch!** Now NO and YES will switch sides. If you argued YES before, now you will argue NO. Work with your same partner and use your notes. Add any arguments and evidence from the clues and sources. Those *now* arguing YES go first.

When both sides have finished, answer the following:

| *Before* I started this discussion, my opinion was that the Mexican-American War: | *After* this discussion, my opinion is that the Mexican-American War: |
|---|---|
| _____was justified. <br> _____was not justified. | _____was justified. <br> _____was not justified. |

4. **Point of View** Do you all agree on the answer to the Guiding Question?
   • _____ Yes
   • _____ No
   If not, on what points do you all agree?

# Take Notes

**Literacy Skills: Identify Cause and Effect** Use what you have read to complete the chart below. List the causes and effects of Jacksonian Democracy on the nation. The first entry is done for you.

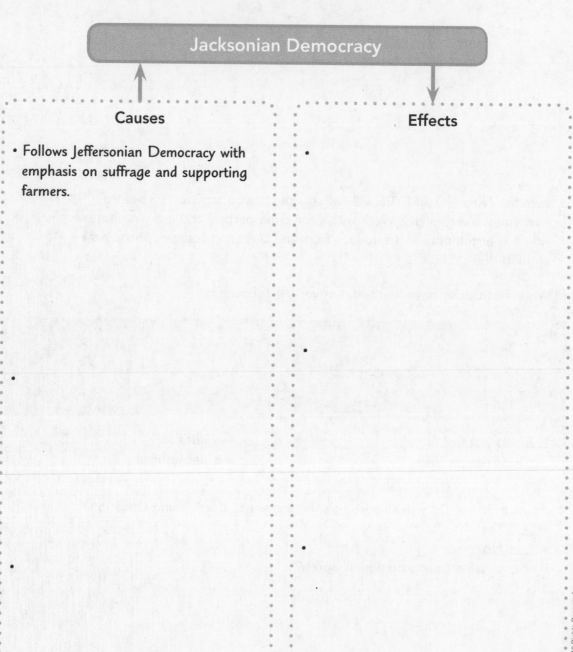

## Jacksonian Democracy

### Causes

- Follows Jeffersonian Democracy with emphasis on suffrage and supporting farmers.

•

•

### Effects

•

•

•

**INTERACTIVE**

For extra help, review the 21st Century Tutorial: **Analyze Cause and Effect**.

# Practice Vocabulary

Sentence Revision **Revise each sentence so that the underlined vocabulary word is used logically. Be sure not to change the vocabulary word. The first one is done for you.**

1. Andrew Jackson's opponents supported the <u>spoils system</u>.
   Andrew Jackson's opponents did not support the <u>spoils system</u>.

2. The spread of political power to the people during Jackson's presidency granted <u>suffrage</u> to women and all males.

3. In the election of 1824, John Quincy Adams won the <u>majority</u> of the popular vote.

4. Members of the <u>Whig Party</u> believed less government involvement improved business pursuits.

5. The <u>Democratic Party</u> platform in the 1830s saw a strong federal government involved in the economy and more privileges for the wealthy as the cornerstone of a strong republic.

## Quick Activity

**American Equality** When Tocqueville arrived in the United States, he wrote, "What struck me during my stay [was] the equality of conditions." Consider the following:

- Tocqueville came from a country where wealthy citizens, or the aristocracy, greatly influenced society.

- Equality at that time in America was different from equality today.

**Team Challenge!** Work with a partner to create a short "quote" of something Tocqueville might say about equality in America today. Write your quote below and on a sticky note to post for the class.

# Take Notes

**Literacy Skills: Compare and Contrast** Use what you have read to compare and contrast the rising sectional differences among the North, West, and South. Fill in the chart below with information about the economy, federal vs. state government, tariffs, and free and slave states. The first entry has been completed for you.

## Rising Sectional Differences

| North | South | West |
|---|---|---|
| **Economy** manufacturing economy | **Economy** agricultural economy; cash crops | **Economy** farming |
| **Federal vs. State Government** | **Federal vs. State Government** | **Federal vs. State Government** |
| **Tariffs** | **Tariffs** | **Tariffs** |
| **Free/Slave States** | **Free/Slave States** | **Free/Slave States** |

👆 **INTERACTIVE**

For extra help, review the 21st Century Tutorial: **Compare and Contrast**.

# Practice Vocabulary

**Vocabulary Quiz Show** Some quiz shows ask a question and expect the contestant to give the answer. In other shows, the contestant is given an answer and must supply the question. If the blank is in the Question column, write the question that would result in the answer in the Answer column. If the question is supplied, write the answer.

| Question | Answer |
|---|---|
| 1. What is a period of severe economic slump and a loss of jobs? | 1. |
| 2. | 2. states' rights |
| 3. At which event did political parties meet to choose candidates for an upcoming election? | 3. |
| 4. | 4. Nullification Act |
| 5. | 5. caucus |

## Take Notes

**Literacy Skills: Cite Evidence** Use what you have read in Lesson 3 to respond to the following statement: **The lives of American Indians were radically changed when settlers arrived.** Fill in the concept web below with evidence from the text that supports the statement. The first entry has been completed for you.

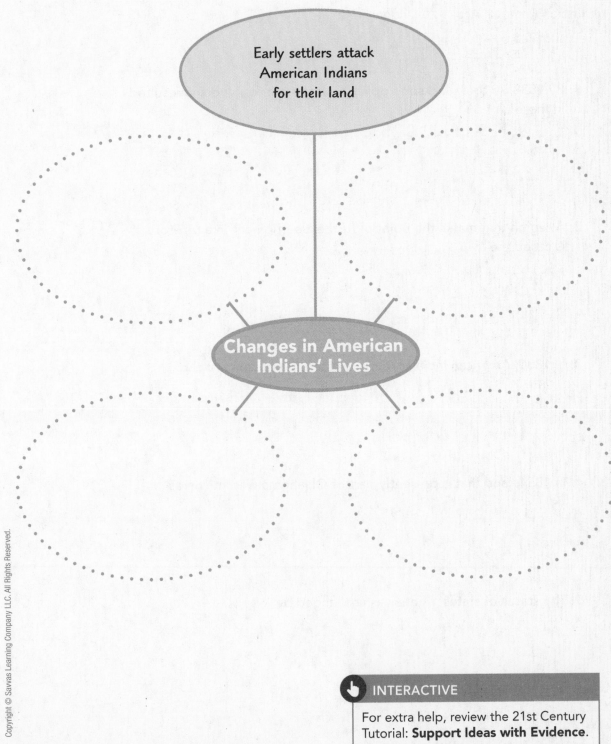

Early settlers attack American Indians for their land

Changes in American Indians' Lives

**INTERACTIVE**

For extra help, review the 21st Century Tutorial: **Support Ideas with Evidence**.

# Practice Vocabulary

**Sentence Builder** Finish the sentences below with a key term from this section. You may have to change the form of the words to complete the sentences.

## Word Bank

frontier                    *Worcester* v. *Georgia*

Indian Removal Act          Indian Territory

Trail of Tears

1. By 1838, Andrew Jackson's policy toward American Indians resulted in the

2. A region that marks the point of furthest settlement in a territory is called the

3. In 1830, American Indian groups resisted the passage of the

4. In 1854, land that is presently part of Oklahoma was known as

5. The status of states' rights was challenged by

## Take Notes

**Literacy Skills: Classify and Categorize** Use what you have read to complete the table below about the westward movement. The first entry has been completed for you.

| Moving Westward | | |
|---|---|---|
| **New territories** | **Why people moved there** | **Life in the West** |
| **Oregon country** | Northwest Ordinance opens up opportunities to buy and settle land | farming |
| **Missouri territory** | | |
| **Texas** | | |
| **Land from Mexican cession** | | |

**INTERACTIVE**

For extra help, review the 21st Century Tutorial: **Categorize**.

# Practice Vocabulary

**True or False?** Decide whether each statement below is true or false. Circle T or F, and then explain your answer. Be sure to include the underlined vocabulary word in your explanation. The first one is done for you.

1. **T / F** As the first steam-powered boats, <u>flatboats</u> helped to revolutionize travel and trade.
   False: <u>Flatboats</u> were not steam powered and were used to transport wagons and people along rivers.

2. **T / F** The <u>National Road</u> was the first step in a federal government-funded transportation system.

3. **T / F** The Constitution states that all <u>revenue</u> or income collected by the government should originate in the House of Representatives.

4. **T / F** As canals became important in American travel, *Clermont* became the first canal for transporting goods.

5. **T / F** In spite of high expectations, the <u>Erie Canal</u> failed to improve water transportation and trade between New York City and Buffalo, New York.

# Take Notes

**Literacy Skills: Summarize** Use what you have read to complete the outline below. For each main idea, provide the details needed to write a summary of the topic. The main idea and details for the first entry have been completed for you.

## Settling Oregon

I. Exploring the territory
    a. geography
    b. weather
    c. how the land was explored

II. Who came to the area?

    a.

    b.

    c.

III. The fur trade

    a.

    b.

IV. Negotiations with Britain

    a.

**INTERACTIVE**

For extra help, review the 21st Century Tutorial: **Summarize**.

## Practice Vocabulary

**Use a Word Bank**  Choose one term from the word bank to fill in each blank. When you have finished, you will have a short summary of important ideas from the section.

### Word Bank

Oregon Country            mountain men

Oregon Trail              rugged individualists

Between 1800 and 1840, thousands of settlers poured into

............................................. . While the rich, virgin soil drew many,

there was also a prosperous fur trade. Fur companies often hired fur

trappers who became known as ............................................. . Many

people admired them as ............................................. . When the fur

trade declined, many ............................................. hired themselves

out as guides along the ............................................. .

## Take Notes

**Literacy Skills: Sequence** Use what you have read to complete the flowchart below. In each space, write the events that led to the independence of Texas. The first event is filled in for you.

**Independence of Texas**

In 1830, Mexico tightens control over Texas.

👆 **INTERACTIVE**

For extra help, review the 21st Century Tutorial: **Sequence**.

# Practice Vocabulary

**Words in Context** For each question below, write an answer that shows your understanding of the **boldfaced** key term.

1. Why was the **Alamo** significant?

2. How did Santa Anna's actions as a **dictator** spark the Texas fight for independence?

3. Why did **missions** continue to spread throughout California?

4. Why were **vaqueros** a part of California tradition?

5. How did the **Santa Fe trail** affect trade routes in the United States?

6. Why is the thirteen-day **seige** of the Alamo significant?

7. Who were the **Puebloans**?

8. How did missions in California become **self-sufficient**?

# Take Notes

**Literacy Skills: Identify Cause and Effect** Use what you have read to complete the chart below. In each box, write the effects of the expansion of the West between 1840 and 1870. The first entry is done for you.

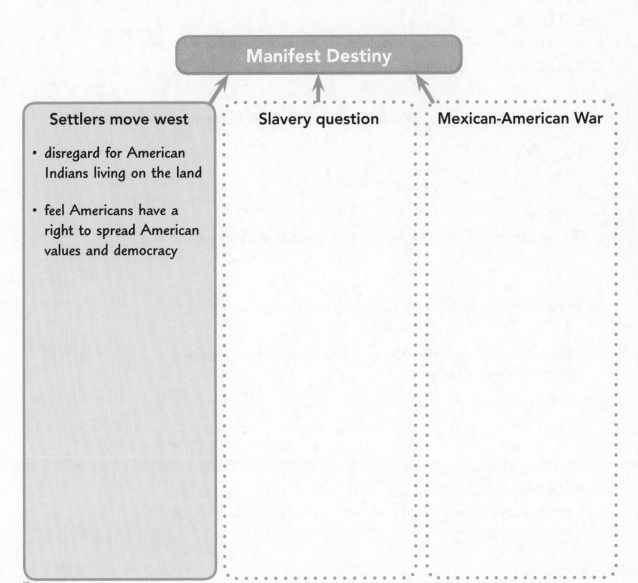

**Manifest Destiny**

**Settlers move west**

- disregard for American Indians living on the land

- feel Americans have a right to spread American values and democracy

**Slavery question**

**Mexican-American War**

 **INTERACTIVE**

For extra help, review the 21st Century Tutorial: **Analyze Cause and Effect**.

# Practice Vocabulary

**Sentence Builder** Finish the sentences below with a key term from this section. You may have to change the form of the words to complete the sentences.

## Word Bank

| | | |
|---|---|---|
| Manifest Destiny | Bear Flag Republic | Treaty of Guadalupe-Hidalgo |
| Mexican Cession | forty-niner | |

**1.** These gold seekers, who rushed to California in 1849, became known as

**2.** The recognition of Texas as part of the United States was part of

**3.** After James Polk's election, the goal of expansion became the government policy known as

**4.** Present-day California, Nevada, Utah, most of Arizona, parts of New Mexico, Colorado, Wyoming, and Texas became part of the United States in the

**5.** Rebels, led by John C. Fremont, declared California independent of Mexico and called their new land the

# Quick Activity The Importance of Water

With a partner, study the photo of the miners seeking gold during the California Gold Rush. What does it tell you about water shortages in the West?

**Team Challenge!** With your partner, draw a picture showing other effects of water shortages on the West. Post your drawing to share with the class. Explain the message behind your drawing.

# Writing Workshop Narrative Essay

As you read, build a response to this prompt: **It is 1844 and your family has decided to move to Oregon. Write a journal entry describing the trip.** The prompts below will help walk you through the process.

## Lesson 1 Writing Task: Introduce Characters (See Student Text, page 347)

List the characters who will play important roles in your journal entry and explain why your family has decided to move west.

## Lesson 2 Writing Task: Establish a Setting (See Student Text, page 358)

Describe the trail from your point of view. How does the setting affect your experiences?

## Lesson 3 Writing Task: Organize Sequence of Events (See Student Text, page 367)

Anecdotes are short, amusing or interesting stories about an incident or person. Create an outline for your journal entry. Start with the planning of your trip. Then identify three anecdotes you could tell about your family's trip.

Planning for Trip

Anecdotes

## Lessons 4 and 5 Writing Tasks: Narrative Techniques

(See Student Text, pages 374 and 381)

A good journal entry will use narrative techniques—such as dialogue, description, and similes—to make it more lively and interesting to read. Identify a narrative technique, and write a sentence based on the lesson's content that uses that technique.

## Lesson 6 Writing Task: Descriptive Details and Sensory Language

(See Student Text, page 391)

Choose one of your anecdotes. Is it interesting enough? Rewrite it, adding descriptive details or sensory language.

## Lesson 7 Writing Task: Strong Conclusion (See Student Text, page 401)

How will your journal entry end? Draft an ending for your entry that will be memorable for your readers.

## Writing Task (See Student Text, page 403)

Using the characters, setting, and anecdotes you've identified, write a journal entry about your family's trip to Oregon. Be sure to use narrative techniques, descriptive details, and sensory language in your writing. Capture the readers' attention in your opening, and end with a strong conclusion to your entry.

## Essential Question Why is culture important?

Before you begin this topic, think about the Essential Question by completing the following activity.

1. Think of one way that music, art, or books have inspired you. Then think of one song, piece of art, or book that an artist created because of something happening in the world. For example, *Uncle Tom's Cabin* is a novel by Harriet Beecher Stowe that was inspired by the evils of slavery.

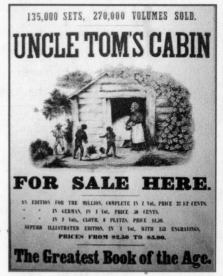

135,000 SETS, 270,000 VOLUMES SOLD.

**UNCLE TOM'S CABIN**

**FOR SALE HERE.**

AN EDITION FOR THE MILLION, COMPLETE IN 1 Vol. PRICE 37 1-2 CENTS.
IN GERMAN, IN 1 Vol. PRICE 50 CENTS.
IN 2 Vols., CLOTH, 6 PLATES, PRICE $1.50.
SUPERB ILLUSTRATED EDITION, IN 1 Vol. WITH 153 ENGRAVINGS.
PRICES FROM $2.50 TO $5.00.

**The Greatest Book of the Age.**

**The [song, art, book] inspired me to**

**The [song, art, book] was inspired by**

## Timeline Skills

As you read, write and/or draw at least three events from the topic. Draw a line from each event to its correct position on the timeline.

| 1810 | 1820 | 1830 |

# Map Skills

Using maps throughout the topic, label the outline map showing the various travel times from New York City. Then, create a key for each of the various travel times and use the key to color the map.

| 1 day, 1857 | 1 week, 1857 | 4 weeks, 1857 |
| 1 day, 1800 | 1 week, 1800 | 4 weeks, 1800 |

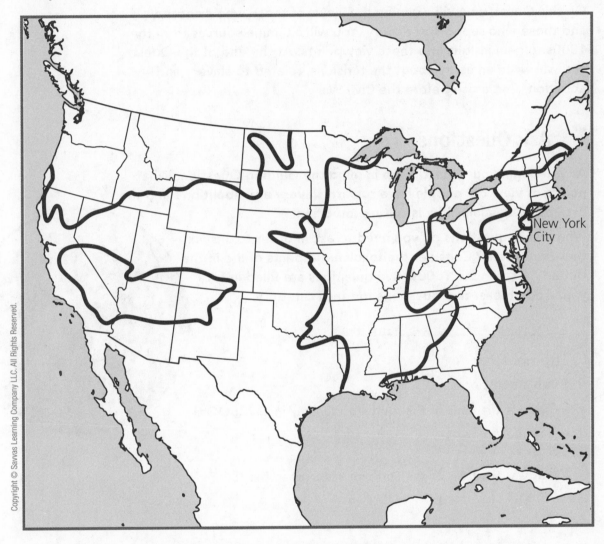

New York City

| 1840 | 1850 | 1860 | 1880 |

# Quest

**Document-Based Writing Inquiry**

# Slavery and Abolition

On this Quest, you will examine the views of those who opposed and those who supported slavery. You will examine sources from the 1800s to gain insight into these viewpoints. At the end of the Quest, you will write an essay about the tensions, related to slavery and abolition, that arose before the Civil War.

## 1 Ask Questions (See Student Text, page 408)

As you begin your Quest, keep in mind the Guiding Question: **What points of view did people have toward slavery and abolition?** and the Essential Question: **Why is culture important?**

What other questions do you need to ask in order to answer these questions? Consider the following aspects of life in the United States in the 1800s. Two questions are filled in for you. Add at least two questions for each category.

**Theme** Economy

Sample questions:

What was the basis of the southern economy in the 1800s?

What was the basis of the northern economy in the 1800s?

**Theme** Culture

**Theme** History

**Theme** New Inventions and Technology

**Theme** My Additional Questions

👆 INTERACTIVE

For extra help with Step 1, review the
21st Century Tutorial: **Ask Questions**.

# Quest CONNECTIONS

## 2 Investigate

As you read about society and culture before the Civil War, collect five connections from your text to help you answer the Guiding Question. Three connections are already chosen for you.

## Connect to the Abolition Movement

**Lesson 2** African Americans Face Discrimination (See Student Text, page 429)

Here's a connection! Look at this section in your text. Who were William Whipper and John Russwurm? What do the accomplishments of these men reveal about the lives of free African Americans in the North in the mid-1800s?

What position do you think men such as Whipper and Russwurm took toward slavery?

# Connect to the South's Economic Dependence

## Lesson 3 Reliance on Plantation Agriculture (See Student Text, page 435)

Here's another connection! What does this section of the text tell you about the interaction between the southern and northern economies? On what was the southern economy based?

How might this situation have influenced the South's views on slavery?

# Connect to Opponents of Slavery

## Lesson 4 How Did Abolitionism Gain Momentum? (See Student Text, page 445)

What does this connection tell you about the two groups of people who oppose slavery?

What clue can you find in this section about how the abolitionists were received by those who supported slavery?

It's Your Turn!  Find two more connections. Fill in the title of your connections, then answer the questions. Connections may be images, primary sources, maps, or text.

## Your Choice | Connect to

### Location in text

What is the main idea of this connection?


What does it tell you about the differing viewpoints in the United States toward slavery and abolition?


## Your Choice | Connect to

### Location in text

What is the main idea of this connection?


What does it tell you about the differing viewpoints in the United States toward slavery and abolition?

## 3 Examine Primary Sources (See Student Text, page 472)

Examine the primary and secondary sources provided online or from your teacher. Fill in the chart to show how these sources demonstrate points of view on both sides of the slavery issue. The first one is completed for you.

| Source | Point of View |
|---|---|
| British Anti-Slavery Society Medallion, 1795 | Abolition/Anti-slavery |
| "No Compromise With the Evil of Slavery" | |
| "Inhumanity of Slavery" | |
| The Southern Address of 1849 | |
| 1837 Broadside | |
| *Cannibals All! Or, Slaves Without Masters* | |

> **INTERACTIVE**
>
> For extra help with Step 3, review the 21st Century Tutorials: **Analyze Primary and Secondary Sources** and **Compare and Contrast**.

## ④ **Write Your Essay** (See Student Text, page 472)

Now it's time to put together all of the information you have gathered and use it to write your essay.

1. **Prepare to Write** You have collected connections and explored primary and secondary sources that show the conflicting points of view about slavery held by Americans in the 1800s. Look through your notes and summarize these viewpoints. Record them here.

**Viewpoints on Slavery and Abolition**

2. **Write a Draft** Using evidence from the clues you found and the documents you explored, write a draft of your essay. Introduce the various viewpoints you have identified, then describe the cultural differences and personal attitudes behind them. Be sure to use vivid details that spring from evidence in the documents you've studied in this Quest.

3. **Share with a Partner** Exchange your draft with a partner. Tell your partner what you like about his or her draft and suggest any improvements.

4. **Finalize Your Essay** Revise your essay. Correct any grammatical or spelling errors. Be sure you have clearly described what you learned from the documents and how you used evidence from them to support your main points.

5. **Reflect on the Quest** Think about your experience completing this topic's Quest. What did you learn about the differing viewpoints on slavery and abolition? What questions do you still have about these views? How will you answer them?

## Reflections

AM I NOT A MAN AND A BROTHER

**INTERACTIVE**

For extra help with Step 4, review the 21st Century Tutorial: **Write an Essay**.

# Take Notes

**Literacy Skills: Cite Evidence** Use what you have read to complete the table. In the first column, write one conclusion from the text. In the second column, write any evidence you can find in the text that supports this conclusion. The first one has been completed for you.

| Conclusions | Evidence |
| --- | --- |
| New machines transformed the textile industry in England. | • In 1764, James Hargreaves developed the spinning jenny, allowing workers to spin several threads at once.<br>• In the 1780s, Edmund Cartwright built a loom powered by water that allowed a worker to produce a great deal more cloth in a day than was possible before. |
| | |
| | |
| | |
| | |

**INTERACTIVE**

For extra help, review the 21st Century Tutorial: **Support Ideas with Evidence**.

# Practice Vocabulary

True or False? Decide whether each statement below is true or false. Circle T or F, and then explain your answer. Be sure to include the underlined vocabulary word in your explanation. The first one is done for you.

1. **T / F** The <u>Industrial Revolution</u> was a fight between factory workers and wealthy factory owners.

   False; The <u>Industrial Revolution</u> was a long, slow process that completely changed the way goods were produced and where people lived and worked.

2. **T / F** Setting up a new business requires <u>capital</u>, or money for investment.

3. **T / F** A <u>capitalist</u> is a person who is trained to use new technologies, such as the spinning jenny and water-powered loom.

4. **T / F** When factories cannot get enough raw materials, the supply of goods drops. <u>Supply</u> is the amount of goods available to sell.

5. **T / F** A large amount of goods, known as <u>scarcity</u>, causes prices to rise.

6. **T / F** Eli Whitney's idea of <u>interchangeable parts</u> meant that the parts of an object could be sold for a low price.

7. **T / F** The young women from nearby farms who came to work in the Lowell mills came to be called the <u>Lowell girls</u>.

8. **T / F** As industry grew, many people left farms for work in city factories, causing less <u>urbanization</u>.

# Take Notes

**Literacy Skills: Identify Main Ideas** Use what you have read to complete the table. Use the details to identify the main idea. The first one has been completed for you.

| What Changes Did the Age of Steam Power Bring? | How Did Workers Respond to Challenges? | How Did Ethnic Minorities Fare in the North? |
|---|---|---|
| **Main Idea:** The harnessing of steam power transformed many aspects of life in the United States. | **Main Idea:** | **Main Idea:** |
| **Details:** Rail lines spread across the country. Factories also began to use steam, resulting in the expansion of industry and more affordable goods. Industrialization improved the standard of living. | **Details:** | **Details:** |

| A Reaction Against Immigrants | African Americans Face Discrimination |
|---|---|
| **Main Idea:** | **Main Idea:** |
| **Details:** | **Details:** |

**INTERACTIVE**

For extra help, review the 21st Century Tutorial: **Identify Main Ideas and Details**.

# Practice Vocabulary

**Vocabulary Quiz Show** Some quiz shows ask a question and expect the contestant to give the answer. In other shows, the contestant is given an answer and must supply the question. If the blank is in the Question column, write the question that would result in the answer in the Answer column. If the question is supplied, write the answer.

| Question | Answer |
|---|---|
| 1. What is another term for a skilled worker? | 1. |
| 2. | 2. famine |
| 3. | 3. discrimination |
| 4. What action, in which workers refused to do their jobs until their demands were met, was illegal in many parts of the country in the early 1800s? | 4. |
| 5. | 5. Know-Nothing Party |
| 6. | 6. nativists |
| 7. What groups were formed when artisans united to protest poor working conditions and low wages? | 7. |

## Take Notes

**Literacy Skills: Compare and Contrast** Use what you have read to complete the charts comparing and contrasting aspects of life in the South. The first one has been completed for you.

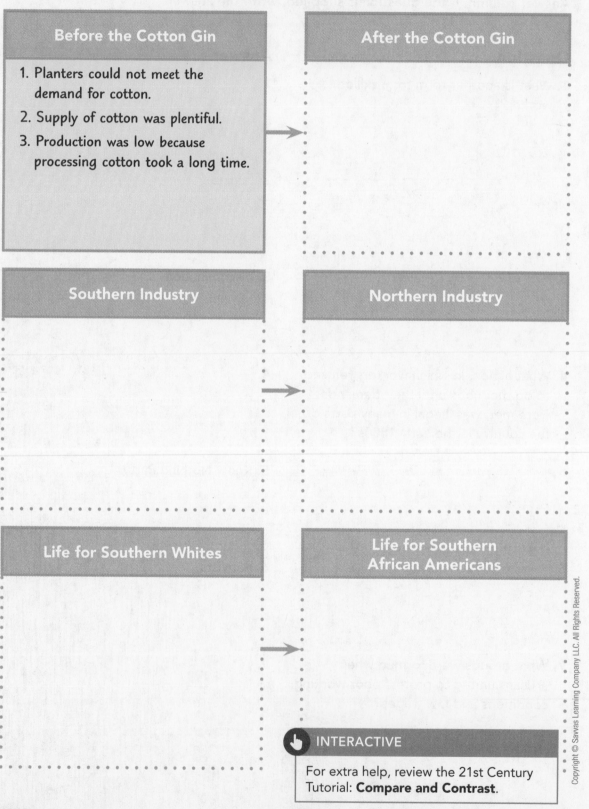

**Before the Cotton Gin**

1. Planters could not meet the demand for cotton.
2. Supply of cotton was plentiful.
3. Production was low because processing cotton took a long time.

**After the Cotton Gin**

**Southern Industry**

**Northern Industry**

**Life for Southern Whites**

**Life for Southern African Americans**

👆 INTERACTIVE

For extra help, review the 21st Century Tutorial: **Compare and Contrast**.

# Practice Vocabulary

**Matching Logic** Using your knowledge of the underlined vocabulary words, draw a line from each sentence in Column 1 to match it with the sentence in Column 2 to which it logically belongs.

| Column 1 | Column 2 |
|---|---|
| 1. The views and way of life of the "<u>cottonocracy</u>" dominated the South. | Before planting, farmers must prepare the land. |
| 2. This idea of the <u>extended family</u> had its roots in Africa. | Swift growth in cotton production meant that by 1850, planters were producing more than 2 million bales of cotton a year. |
| 3. Under the <u>slave codes</u>, enslaved African Americans could not leave their owner's land without a written pass. | These wealthy planter families lived mainly in the cotton belt of the lowland South and in coastal areas of South Carolina, Georgia, and Louisiana. |
| 4. The invention of the cotton gin meant that planters needed more land to <u>cultivate</u>. | They were designed to keep enslaved African Americans from running away or rebelling. |
| 5. Slavery spread as a result of the cotton <u>boom</u>. | Grandparents, parents, children, aunts, uncles, and cousins formed a close-knit group. |

# Take Notes

**Literacy Skills: Summarize** Use what you have read to complete the
table. In each space, write an important point related to that topic.
Then summarize the lesson. The first one has been completed for you.

| What Form Did Early Opposition to Slavery Take? | How Did Abolitionism Gain Momentum? | Who Opposed the Abolitionists? |
|---|---|---|
| **Slavery in the 1800s** Slavery was gradually ended in the North; religious beliefs led some to oppose slavery; slavery was banned in the Northwest Territory. | Abolitionists | Northerners Against Abolition |
| **The Colonization Movement** The American Colonization Society proposed to end slavery by setting up an independent colony in Africa for Africans and African Americans. | Civil Disobedience and the Underground Railroad  *Uncle Tom's Cabin* | Southerners Defend Slavery Against the North |

Summary:

**INTERACTIVE**

For extra help, review the 21st Century
Tutorial: **Summarize**.

# Practice Vocabulary

**Sentence Builder** Finish the sentences below with a vocabulary term from this section. You may have to change the form of the words to complete the sentences.

## Word Bank

American Colonization Society

*The Liberator*

civil disobedience

abolitionist

Underground Railroad

1. A person who wanted to end slavery in the United States was known as a(n)

   :.................................................:

2. "Conductors" guided runaways to "stations" where they could spend the night on the

   :.................................................:

3. Disobeying laws that one feels are unjust is known as

   :.................................................:

4. The group that President Monroe helped to set up a colony in western Africa was called the

   :.................................................:

5. William Lloyd Garrison called his antislavery newspaper

   :.................................................:

## Quick Activity Abolitionists Speak Out

With a partner or small group, examine this 1859 flyer announcing the sale of enslaved people.

**NEGROES**

## FOR SALE.

I will sell by Public Auction, on Tuesday of next Court, being the 29th of November, *Eight Valuable Family Servants*, consisting of one Negro Man, a first-rate field hand, one No. 1 Boy, 17 years o' age, a trusty house servant, one excellent Cook, one House-Maid, and one Seamstress. The balance are under 12 years of age. They are sold for no fault, but in consequence of my going to reside North. Also a quantity of Household and Kitchen Furniture, Stable Lot, &c. Terms accommodating, and made known on day of sale.

### Jacob August.

P. J. TURNBULL, *Auctioneer.*

*Warrenton, October 28, 1859.*

Printed at the *News* office, Warrenton, North Carolina.

How might an abolitionist use the information in this flyer to point out some of the evils of slavery? Refer to specific parts of the flyer in your answer.

> *We* do not preach rebellion—no, but submission and peace. Our enemies may accuse us of striving to stir up the slaves to revenge but their accusations are false, and made only to excite the prejudices of the whites, and to destroy our influence. We say, that the possibility of a bloody insurrection at the south fills us with dismay; and we avow, too, as plainly, that if any people were ever justified in throwing off the yoke of their tyrants, the slaves are that people. It is not we, but our guilty countrymen, who put arguments into the mouths, and swords into the hands of the slaves. Every sentence that they write—every word that they speak—every resistance that they make, against foreign oppression, is a call upon their slaves to destroy them. Every Fourth of July celebration must embitter and inflame the minds of the slaves.
>
> — William Lloyd Garrison, Editorial, *The Liberator* (January 8, 1831)

**Team Challenge!** The excerpt above is from an 1831 editorial. An editorial is a newspaper article that gives an opinion on a particular issue. Work with your group to write an editorial about the work of abolitionists that might have appeared in your local newspaper in the 1850s. Find an image from your text or online that you might use to illustrate the editorial, then design the article and illustration to look like a real page from a newspaper.

# Take Notes

**Literacy Skills: Draw Conclusions** Use what you have read to complete the table. In the right column, write conclusions that can be drawn from the information in the box to the left. The first one has been completed for you.

| Main Idea | Conclusion |
|---|---|
| Reformers fought to end slavery, increase access to education, improve conditions in prisons, expand women's rights, and more. | Conflict likely erupted between reformers and those who wanted things to stay as they were. |
| Women often played a leading role in reform movements. | |
| By the 1850s, most northern states had set up free tax-supported elementary schools. | |
| Women had few legal or political rights at this time. | |
| The *Declaration of Sentiments* was modeled on the Declaration of Independence. | |
| Women won new opportunities in education and employment. | |

**INTERACTIVE**

For extra help, review the 21st Century Tutorial: **Draw Conclusions**.

# Practice Vocabulary

**Use a Word Bank** Choose one word from the word bank to fill in each blank. When you have finished, you will have a short summary of important ideas from the section.

## Word Bank

social reform

debtors

Seneca Falls Convention

women's rights movement

temperance movement

Second Great Awakening

Some Americans saw many things that needed to be fixed during the Era

of Reform. Dorothea Dix convinced state prison systems to stop cruel

punishment and the treatment of ........................................ as

criminals. Those who took part in the ........................................

urged people to drink less alcohol or stop drinking altogether. Much of

the impulse toward ........................................ at this time had its

roots in the ........................................ that swept the nation. This

movement taught that people could save their souls by their actions.

Inspired by religion and their work on other causes, women met at the

........................................ in 1848 to discuss equal rights for

women. This meeting was the beginning of the long- and still-continuing

........................................ .

# Quick Activity  An Echo Across Time

**In 1776, the founders of the United States declared their independence from Britain with these ringing words:**

> . . . The history of the present King of Great Britain is a history of repeated injuries and usurpations, all having in direct object the establishment of an absolute Tyranny over these States. To prove this, let Facts be submitted to a candid world.
>
> He has refused his Assent to Laws, the most wholesome and necessary for the public good.
>
> He has forbidden his Governors to pass Laws of immediate and pressing importance.
>
> —The Declaration of Independence (1776)

**More than seventy years later, the women who attended the Seneca Falls Convention declared their own independence. Underline words and phrases that are the same in the two declarations.**

> The history of mankind is a history of repeated injuries and usurpations on the part of man toward woman, having in direct object the establishment of an absolute tyranny over her. To prove this, let facts be submitted to a candid world.
>
> He has never permitted her to exercise her inalienable right to the elective franchise.
>
> He has compelled her to submit to laws, in the formation of which she had no voice.
>
> —The Declaration of Sentiments and Resolutions, 1848

**Team Challenge!  With a partner or small group, explore the similarities between the Declaration of Independence and the Declaration of Sentiments. Then answer this question: Why do you think the writers of the Declaration of Sentiments chose to model their work on the earlier document?**

## Take Notes

**Literacy Skills: Identify Cause and Effect** Use what you have read to complete the diagrams. Two causes have been completed for you.

**Effect: By the mid-1800s, Americans developed a new pride in their country and its culture.**

**Cause**

The Hudson River School and other artists painted scenes of American life and American landscapes.

**Cause**

**Cause**

**Effect: Henry David Thoreau writes about civil disobedience.**

**Cause**

Transcendentalism develops.

**Cause**

**Cause**

**INTERACTIVE**

For extra help, review the 21st Century Tutorial: **Analyze Cause and Effect**.

# Practice Vocabulary

**Word Map** Study the word map for the term *Hudson River School*. Characteristics are words or phrases that relate to the term in the center of the word map. Non-characteristics are words and phrases not associated with that term. Use the blank word map to explore the meaning of the word *transcendentalist*. Then make a word map of your own for the word *individualism*.

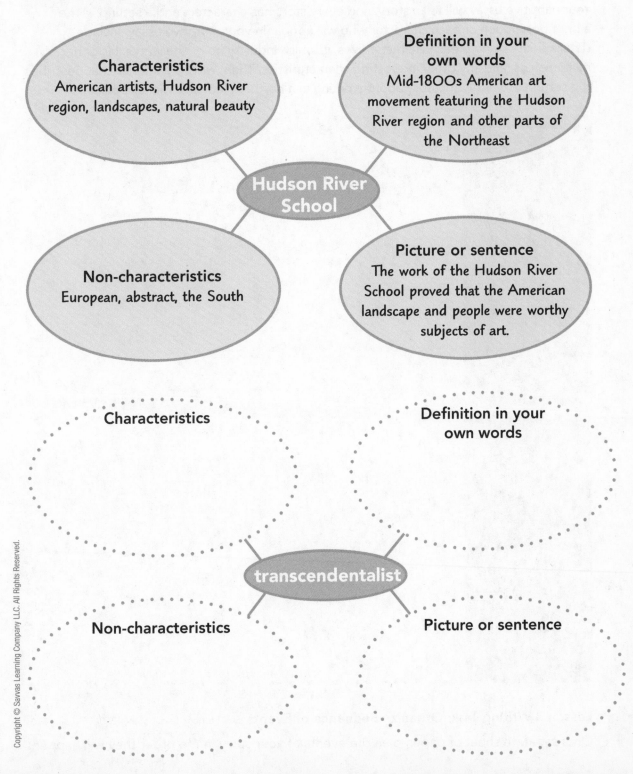

**Characteristics**
American artists, Hudson River region, landscapes, natural beauty

**Definition in your own words**
Mid-1800s American art movement featuring the Hudson River region and other parts of the Northeast

**Hudson River School**

**Non-characteristics**
European, abstract, the South

**Picture or sentence**
The work of the Hudson River School proved that the American landscape and people were worthy subjects of art.

**Characteristics**

**Definition in your own words**

**transcendentalist**

**Non-characteristics**

**Picture or sentence**

# Writing Workshop  Narrative Essay

As you read, build a response to this topic: **Write a three-paragraph narrative essay from the point of view of a young person working in northern industry during this time period.** The prompts below will help walk you through the process.

## Lessons 1 and 2 Writing Tasks: Introduce Characters and Establish Setting
(See Student Text, pages 420 and 430)

Your narrative essay will tell a story, and every story has characters and a setting. Write a brief description of each character who will appear in your narrative essay. Include details such as where each character lives, in which industry he or she works, his or her relationships, and any other interesting characteristics. Then, write a sentence that describes the setting in which your story about working in a northern industry will take place.

Character 1

Character 2

Character 3

Setting

## Lesson 3 Writing Task: Organize Sequence of Events (See Student Text, page 442)

On a separate sheet of paper, plan the events of your story in the order they will happen.

**Lessons 4 and 5 Writing Tasks: Use Narrative Techniques, Descriptive Details, and Sensory Language** (See Student Text, pages 449 and 463)

Will you tell your story using the first person point of view—"I lived . . ." or "I saw . . ."? Or the third person—"He lived . . ." or "He saw . . ."? Will you use present or past tense? Will you include dialogue? After deciding these points, think about how to bring your story to life. Write some descriptive words and sensory language about where you are sitting right now. Then, write descriptive words and sensory language related to your story.

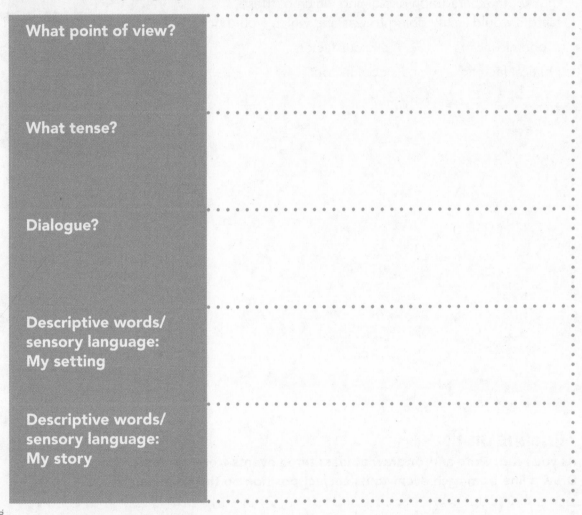

| What point of view? | |
| What tense? | |
| Dialogue? | |
| Descriptive words/ sensory language: My setting | |
| Descriptive words/ sensory language: My story | |

**Lesson 6 Writing Task: Prepare a Final Draft** (See Student Text, page 471)

Using the details you have fleshed out here, write a first draft of your story. After you have finished, review your work. Check your structure, spelling, and grammar, and prepare a final draft.

**Writing Task** (See Student Text, page 473)

Read your final draft. Does the story follow the plan you set out here? Does it accurately describe life for a young person working in a northern industry during the Industrial Revolution? Once you are satisfied with your work, trade essays with a partner. Make any corrections or improvements your partner suggests.

# 8 Sectionalism and Civil War Preview

## Essential Question **When is war justified?**

**Before you begin this topic, think about the Essential Question by completing the following activity.**

1. What factors justify going to war? Read the list below, then write a paragraph explaining which of these factors would justify going to war and which would not.

economic factors                    religious factors

political factors                    social factors

## Timeline Skills

**As you read, write and/or draw at least three events from the topic. Draw a line from each event to its correct position on the timeline.**

| 1820 | 1830 | 1840 |
|------|------|------|

# Map Skills

Using maps throughout the topic, add the state abbreviations for those states that are missing labels. Then use different colors to shade the Union states, the Border states, the Confederate states, and the territories.

| | | | |
|---|---|---|---|
| California | Georgia | Kansas | Kentucky |
| Mississippi | New York | Ohio | South Carolina |
| Texas | Virginia | West Virginia | |

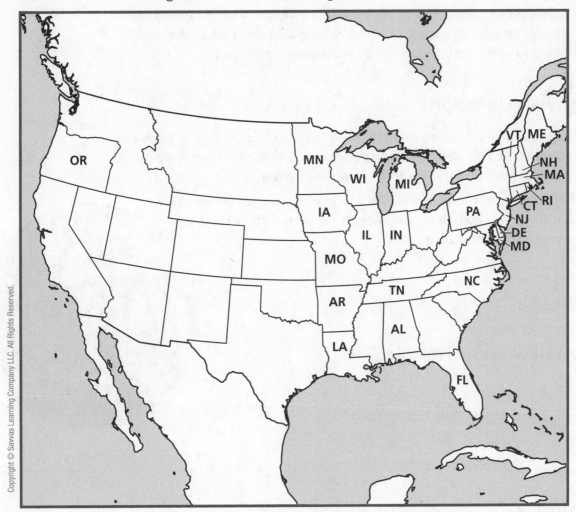

| 1850 | 1860 | 1870 |
|---|---|---|

# Quest

## Project-Based Learning Inquiry

## A Lincoln Website

On this Quest, you need to compare Abraham Lincoln's writings and speeches to the Declaration of Independence. You will examine sources from Lincoln's speeches and writings. At the end of the Quest, you will create a website to share your findings.

### 1 Ask Questions (See Student Text, page 478)

As you begin your Quest, keep in mind the Guiding Question: **How did Abraham Lincoln's writings and speeches relate to the Declaration of Independence?** and the Essential Question: **When is war justified?**

What other questions do you need to ask in order to answer these questions? Two questions are filled in for you. Add at least two questions for each category.

---

**Theme** The Gettysburg Address

Sample questions:

What was the Gettysburg Address?


Why is it memorable?

---

**Theme** The Declaration of Independence

**Theme** Preserving the Union

**Theme** Election of 1864

**Theme** My Additional Questions

 INTERACTIVE

For extra help with Step 1, review the 21st Century Tutorial: **Ask Questions**.

# Quest CONNECTIONS

## 2 Investigate

As you read about President Lincoln and the Civil War, collect five connections from your text to help you answer the Guiding Question. Three connections are already chosen for you.

## Connect to the Lincoln/Douglas Debates

**Lesson 2** How Did Abraham Lincoln Come to Lead the Republican Party? (See Student Text, page 497)

Here's a connection! Find the passage in the Declaration of Independence that explains the rights that all men should have. How do Lincoln's comments during his series of debates with Stephen Douglas support the ideas expressed in the Declaration of Independence?

What were Stephen Douglas's views on popular sovereignty? What were Lincoln's views?

# Connect to the Right to Alter or to Abolish

**Lesson 3** A Move Toward Civil War (See Student Text, page 503)

Here's another connection! What does the Declaration of Independence say about the people's displeasure with their current government?

What does Lincoln say about this in his speeches?

Secessionists leaving the Union.

# Connect to the Emancipation Proclamation

**Primary Source** Abraham Lincoln, The Emancipation Proclamation
(See Student Text, page 531)

What does the Declaration of Independence say about the responsibility of government to protect the safety and happiness of the people?

How is this passage in the Declaration of Independence reflected in the Emancipation Proclamation?

It's Your Turn! **Find two more connections. Fill in the title of your connections, then answer the questions. Connections may be images, primary sources, maps, or text.**

## Your Choice | Connect to

### Location in text
What is the main idea of this connection?

What does it tell you about Lincoln's understanding of the Declaration of Independence?

## Your Choice | Connect to

### Location in text
What is the main idea of this connection?

What does it tell you about Lincoln's understanding of the Declaration of Independence?

## ③ Conduct Research (See Student Text, page 544)

Examine Abraham Lincoln's Emancipation Proclamation in your text. Then find additional writings and speeches from Lincoln in the text or online. List these additional sources in the chart and then note how they reveal the ways that Lincoln's speeches and writings relate to the Declaration of Independence. The first one is completed for you.

| Abraham Lincoln's Writings/Speeches | Relation to the Declaration of Independence |
|---|---|
| Emancipation Proclamation (1863) | "All men are created equal," including enslaved people. Government is responsible for protecting the rights of all people, including the enslaved. |
| | |
| | |
| | |

👆 **INTERACTIVE**

For extra help with Step 3, review the 21st Century Tutorial: **Analyze Primary and Secondary Sources**.

## ④ Create a Website (See Student Text, page 544)

Now is the time to put together all of the information you have gathered and use it to create your two-page website. Work with a partner or team. Familiarize yourself with digital tools and software to help you create images and text for your website.

1. **Prepare to Write** You have collected connections and explored primary sources that show how Lincoln's speeches and writings reflected ideas in the Declaration of Independence. Look through your notes and decide which speeches and writings you want to highlight on your website. Record them here. Then, decide which team member will write and design each section of your website.

### Lincoln's Writings and Speeches

**2. Write a Draft** Using evidence from the clues you found and the documents you explored, write a draft of your section of the website, including any visuals you plan to use.

**3. Share with a Partner** Exchange your draft with a partner. Tell your partner what you like about his or her draft and suggest any improvements.

**4. Finalize Your Plans for Your Website.** Make any revisions needed. Are your explanations clear? Do your images relate well to your content? Once you finalize your plans, create your website.

**5. Reflect on the Quest** Think about your experience completing this topic's Quest. What did you learn about Abraham Lincoln and his admiration for the ideas in the Declaration of Independence? What questions do you still have about his writings and how they reflect ideas in the Declaration of Independence? How will you answer them?

**Reflections**

**INTERACTIVE**

For extra help with Step 4, review the 21st Century Tutorial: **Evaluate Web Sites**.

# Take Notes

**Literacy Skills: Compare and Contrast** Use what you have learned to complete the Venn diagram. Compare and contrast the Missouri Compromise of 1820 and the Missouri Compromise of 1850. In what ways were the provisions different? In what ways were the provisions the same? The first entry has been completed for you.

**Missouri Compromise 1820**

**Both**

**Missouri Compromise 1850**

Missouri admitted as a slave state.

INTERACTIVE

For extra help, review the 21st Century Tutorial: **Compare and Contrast**.

# Practice Vocabulary

**True or False?** Decide whether each statement below is true or false. Circle T or F, and then explain your answer. Be sure to include the underlined vocabulary word in your explanation. The first one is done for you.

1. **T / F** The <u>Missouri Compromise</u> was a series of laws in 1820 that favored the admission of free states to the Union.
   False; The <u>Missouri Compromise</u> was a series of laws in 1820 and 1850 that maintained a balance between free and slave states admitted to the Union.

2. **T / F** The newly formed <u>Free-Soil Party</u>, whose members were mostly southerners, campaigned for popular sovereignty in the western territories.

3. **T / F** Southerners felt justified in the decision to <u>secede</u> because they said the North did not respect the compact between states as set forth in the Constitution.

4. **T / F** Bleeding Kansas was the result of the repeal of <u>popular sovereignty</u> in Kansas and Nebraska.

5. **T / F** The <u>Compromise of 1850</u> applied to the Louisiana Purchase and the Mexican Cession.

6. **T / F** <u>The Fugitive Slave Act</u> of 1850, with added provisions and heavier punishments, was more harsh than the Fugitive Slave Act passed in 1793.

7. **T / F** Daniel Webster felt the Compromise of 1850 would not prevent <u>civil war</u>.

8. **T / F** Personal liberty laws passed in the North allowed <u>fugitives</u> to argue their cases before a court.

## Take Notes

**Literacy Skills: Identify Cause and Effect** Use what you have learned to complete the chart. Write the effects of each event on the North and on the South. The first one is completed for you.

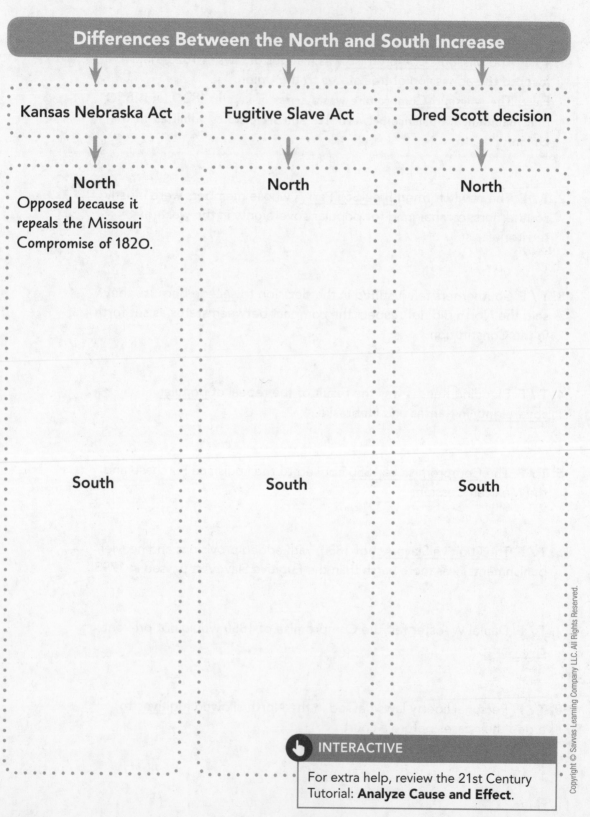

**Differences Between the North and South Increase**

| Kansas Nebraska Act | Fugitive Slave Act | Dred Scott decision |
| --- | --- | --- |
| **North** Opposed because it repeals the Missouri Compromise of 1820. | **North** | **North** |
| **South** | **South** | **South** |

**INTERACTIVE**

For extra help, review the 21st Century Tutorial: **Analyze Cause and Effect**.

# Practice Vocabulary

**Vocabulary Quiz Show** Some quiz shows ask a question and expect the contestant to give the answer. In other shows, the contestant is given an answer and must supply the question. If the blank is in the Question column, write the question that would result in the answer in the Answer column. If the question is supplied, write the answer.

**Question**

1. 

2. What measure did Stephen Douglas propose to organize government in two territories?

3. 

4. What said that Congress did not have the power to ban slavery in the territories?

5. Which proslavery group traveled to the Kansas-Nebraska territory to set up a government?

6. 

7. What organization attracted people who were opposed to the spread of slavery in the western territories?

8. What is it called when informal military groups use hit-and-run tactics?

**Answer**

1. martyr

2. 

3. arsenal

4. 

5. 

6. treason

7. 

8.

## Quick Activity Formerly a Slave

With a partner or small group, read the excerpt below. It is the narrative of an escaped slave, Nancy Howard. Her story is part of a collection of narratives of former slaves who escaped to Canada. The stories were gathered by Boston abolitionist Benjamin Drew.

> I was born in Arundel County, Maryland—was brought up in Baltimore. After my escape, I lived in Lynn, Mass., seven years. But I left there, through fear of being carried back, owing to the fugitive slave law. I have lived in St. Catherines [Ontario, Canada] less than a year.
>
> The way I got away was—my mistress was sick and went into the country for her health. I went to stay with her cousin. After a month, my mistress was sent back to the city to her cousin's and I waited on her. My daughter had been off [successfully escaped] three years. A friend said to me—"Now is your chance to get off." At last I concluded to go—the friend supplying me with money. I was asked no questions on the way north.
>
> —from Benjamin Drew, *The Refugee: Narratives of Fugitive Slaves in Canada Related by Themselves* (1856)

This is one story. Why did Nancy leave Massachusetts? Do you think her fears were justified? Explain your answer.

**Team Challenge!** The picture above shows African Americans arriving at a place where they can live in freedom. How do you think these people feel? If you were an enslaved person planning to escape, would your plans be influenced by the *Dred Scott* decision? Working with your partner or group, write a short narrative from the viewpoint of the enslaved person that tells whether or not you will keep your plans to escape in light of this decision. Share your stories with the class.

 Sectionalism and Civil War

# Take Notes

**Literacy Skills: Compare and Contrast** Use what you have read to complete the tables. List the differences between the North and South during the early years of the Civil War. The first entry is completed for you.

|  | North | South |
|---|---|---|
| **Reason for fighting** | • To preserve the Union | • To preserve their way of life |
| **Advantages** |  |  |
| **Disadvantages** |  |  |

INTERACTIVE

For extra help, review the 21st Century Tutorial: **Compare and Contrast**.

# Practice Vocabulary

**Word Map** Study the word map for the word *unamendable*.
Characteristics are words or phrases that relate to the term in the
center of the word map. Non-characteristics are words and phrases
not associated with that term. Use the blank word map to explore the
meaning of the word *acquiescence*. Then make a word map of your own
for the term *border state*.

**Characteristics**
permanent, unchangeable

**Definition in your
own words**
An addition to the
Constitution that cannot
be changed

**unamendable**

**Non-characteristics**
can be changed

**Picture or sentence**
The unamendable provisions
were a controversial part of the
Crittendon proposal.

**Characteristics**

**Definition in your
own words**

**acquiescence**

**Non-characteristics**

**Picture or sentence**

## Take Notes

**Literacy Skills: Sequence** Use what you have read to complete the
timeline with the five important battles that occurred during 1862.
Then, in the box at bottom, write the significance of each battle.

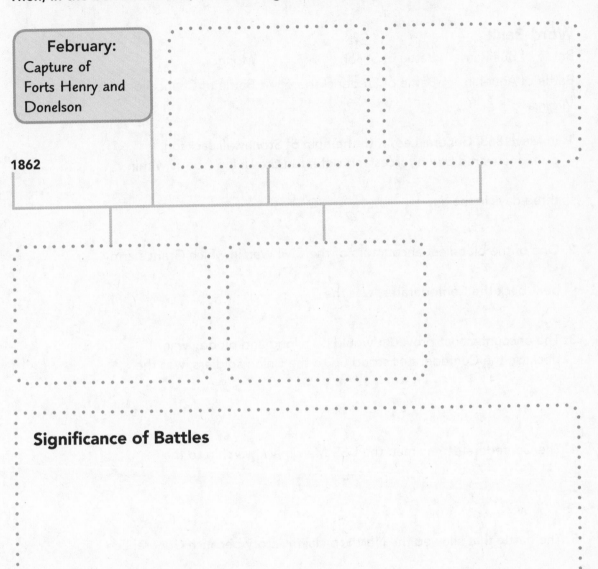

**February:**
Capture of
Forts Henry and
Donelson

1862

**Significance of Battles**

INTERACTIVE

For extra help, review the 21st Century
Tutorial: **Sequence**.

# Practice Vocabulary

**Sentence Builder** Finish the sentences below with a key term from this section. You may have to change the form of the words to complete the sentences.

## Word Bank

| | | |
|---|---|---|
| Battle of Bull Run | Battle of Shiloh | *Monitor* |
| Battle of Antietam | Battle of Fredericksburg | Battle of Chancellorsville |
| *Virginia* | | |

1. In May 1863, General Lee, with the help of Stonewall Jackson, outmaneuvered Union forces and defeated the Union troops within

   three days in the ......................................... .

2. One of the bloodiest encounters of the Civil War, in which Grant's army

   beat back the Confederates, was the ......................................... .

3. The encounter that proved it would be a long and bloody war, because the Confederates stood up to the Union soldiers, was the

   ......................................... .

4. The Confederates renamed the USS *Merrimack* warship to the

   ......................................... .

5. The battle that allowed the North to claim victory because General Lee

   withdrew his troops was the ......................................... .

6. After the Confederates took the *Virginia* out for battle, the Union countered with their own ironclad, called the

   ......................................... .

7. The encounter that was one of the Union's worst defeats, and resulted in Burnside being relieved of command, was the

   ......................................... .

# Take Notes

**Literacy Skills: Summarize** Use what you have read to complete the chart. After you have completed the chart, provide a summary describing how these factors changed or challenged the North and South during the Civil War. The first entry Is completed for you.

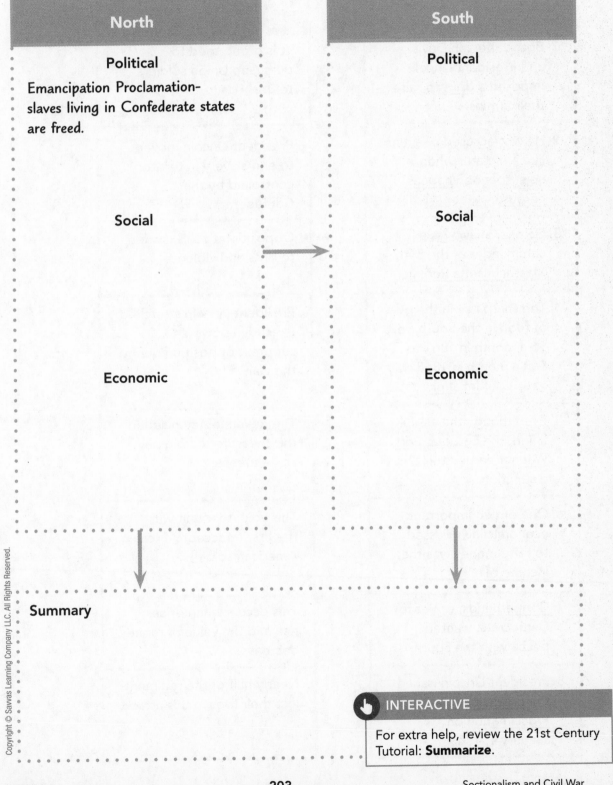

| North | South |
|---|---|
| **Political** | **Political** |
| Emancipation Proclamation- slaves living in Confederate states are freed. | |
| **Social** | **Social** |
| **Economic** | **Economic** |

**Summary**

**INTERACTIVE**

For extra help, review the 21st Century Tutorial: **Summarize**.

# Practice Vocabulary

**Matching Logic** Using your knowledge of the underlined words, draw a line from each sentence in Column 1 to match it with the sentence in Column 2 to which it logically belongs.

| Column 1 | Column 2 |
|---|---|
| 1. Both Jefferson Davis and President Lincoln imposed a <u>draft</u> to raise their armies. | This group tried to persuade Union soldiers to desert. |
| 2. He was accused of acting like a dictator when he suspended <u>habeas corpus</u>. | President Lincoln moved to end slavery in territory controlled by the Confederacy. |
| 3. Colonel Shaw was a commander of the <u>54th Massachusetts Regiment</u>. | Opposition to this law led to riots and violence. |
| 4. The sharp rise in the price of food in the South from $6 a month in 1861 to $68 a month in 1863 was a result of <u>inflation</u>. | President Lincoln stretched executive powers to suppress opposition during the war. |
| 5. Even though the assault failed, the battle at <u>Fort Wagner</u> earned this unit distinction. | The Revenue Act included this measure to help pay war expenses. |
| 6. One of two important economic laws passed to raise money was the <u>income tax</u>. | This volunteer unit was the first to accept African American soldiers. |
| 7. <u>Copperheads</u>, or Peace Democrats, wanted peace with the South. | This occurs when prices rise and the value of money decreases. |
| 8. President Lincoln issued the <u>Emancipation Proclamation</u> on January 1, 1863. | Nearly half of the regiment lost their lives in this attack. |

# Quick Activity Living through the War

As the war moved into its third year, the effect on civilians became more difficult. The account below is from Agnes, who lived in Richmond, Virginia.

> The crowd now rapidly increased and numbered, I am sure more than a thousand women and children. It grew and grew until it reached the dignity of a mob—a bread riot.
>
> —Agnes, quoted in *Reminiscences of Peace and War*

While the account is brief, it still creates a picture in the reader's mind. Working with a partner or a small group, give a one-minute news report of the situation. What do you know about the crowd? What was the mood? Who was affected? Then read the accounts of a soldier's life during the war.

> The first thing in the morning is drill. Then drill, then drill again. Then drill, drill, a little more drill. Then drill and lastly drill.

> Look at our company—21 have died of disease, 18 have become so unhealthy as to be discharged, and only four have been killed in battle.

**Team Challenge!** Working with a partner or a small group, explain how a Civil War correspondent on the front lines and a historian many years later might have used information from these and other primary sources to determine what the life of a soldier was like. What sort of sources would each use? What information might they have learned from these sources? Share your report with the class.

## Lesson 6 The War's End

# Take Notes

**Literacy Skills: Sequence** Use what you have read to complete the flowchart. Identify significant events during the last two years of the war (1863–1865). In the last box, describe the effect of the war on the nation. The first entry is completed for you.

Siege of Vicksburg

Effects of the war

**INTERACTIVE**

For extra help, review the 21st Century Tutorial: **Sequence**.

# Practice Vocabulary

Words in Context For each question below, write an answer that shows your understanding of the boldfaced key term.

1. Why was the meeting at **Appomattox Court House** significant?

2. How did **Pickett's Charge** change the course of the war?

3. Explain what happens during a military **siege**.

4. What happened at the **Battle of Gettysburg**?

5. What was Lincoln's goal in the **Gettysburg Address**?

# Writing Workshop Informative Essay

As you read, build a response to this question: **What were the differences between the North and the South before, during, and after the Civil War?** The prompts below will help you walk through the process.

## Lessons 1 and 2 Writing Tasks: Consider Your Purpose and Pick an Organizing Strategy (See Student Text, pages 487 and 499)

Describe what information you will provide to complete the task. Then, consider how you will present your information. Will you include visuals? Set out your plan below.

## Lesson 3 Writing Task: Develop Your Thesis (See Student Text, pages 511)

Write one sentence that describes your ideas on the differences between the North and the South before, during, and after the Civil War. This will be your thesis statement.

**Lesson 4 Writing Task: Support Thesis with Details** (See Student Text, pages 519)

Review your thesis statement. Make any revisions you feel are necessary. List details from Lessons 1, 2, 3, and 4 describing the differences between the North and South. Use the table below to list these details.

| North | South |
|---|---|
| | |

**Lesson 5 Writing Task: Write an Introduction** (See Student Text, page 530)

Write the opening paragraph of your essay on another piece of paper. This opening paragraph should introduce your thesis and be clear and concise.

**Lesson 6 Writing Task: Draft Your Essay** (See Student Text, page 543)

Use the details you have been gathering to write a first draft of your essay about the differences between the North and South before, during, and after the Civil War.

**Writing Task** (See Student Text, page 545)

Using the draft you created, answer the following question in a five-paragraph informative essay: What were the differences between the North and the South before, during, and after the Civil War?

# The Reconstruction Era Preview

## Essential Question  How should we handle conflict?

Before you begin this topic, think about the Essential Question by answering the following questions.

1. Check the ideas that you think are helpful ways of resolving conflict.

__compromising          __shouting            __speaking kindly

__listening to everyone  __being open-minded   __name-calling

__hitting                __seeing another perspective

2. Preview the topic by skimming lesson titles, headings, and graphics. List ideas that you think might have been sources of conflict after the Civil War.

## Timeline Skills

As you read, write and/or draw at least three events from the topic. Draw a line from each event to its correct position on the timeline.

| 1865 | 1870 |
|------|------|

# Map Skills

**Using maps throughout the topic, label the states listed below. Then, color and number each military district.**

| Alabama | Arkansas | Florida | Georgia |
|---------|----------|---------|---------|
| Louisiana | Mississippi | North Carolina | South Carolina |
| Texas | Virginia | | |

1875        1880

**Civic Discussion Inquiry**

# The End of Reconstruction

On this Quest, in the role of an historian, you will explore sources and gather information about the ending of Reconstruction. Then, you will participate in a civic discussion with other historians about the Guiding Question.

## 1 Ask Questions (See Student Text, page 550)

As you begin your Quest, keep in mind the Guiding Question: **Should the United States have ended Reconstruction in 1877?** and the Essential Question: **How should we handle conflict?**

What other questions do you need to ask in order to answer these questions? Consider themes, such as the conflict that arose during rebuilding, Lincoln's plan, southern Democrats, northern Republicans, and the South and Reconstruction. Two questions are filled in for you. Add at least two questions for each of the other two categories.

**Theme** Rebuilding Brings Conflict

Sample questions:

What plan did white southern Democrats favor for rebuilding the South?


What plan did northern Republicans favor?

**Theme** Lincoln's Plan

**Theme** Southern Democrats

**Theme** Northern Republicans

**Theme** The South and Reconstruction

**Theme** My Additional Questions

 **INTERACTIVE**

For extra help with Step 1, review the
21st Century Tutorial: **Ask Questions**.

## Quest CONNECTIONS

## ② Investigate

As you read about the ending of Reconstruction, collect five connections to help you answer the Guiding Question. Three connections are already chosen for you.

## Connect to Reconstruction Problems

**Lesson 1** The Effects of the Civil War (See Student Text, page 552)

Here's a connection! Read this section in your text. What problems did the country face after the Civil War?

What problems would Reconstruction be expected to solve?

## Connect to Frederick Douglass

**Primary Source** Frederick Douglass, "What the Black Man Wants"
(See Student Text, page 564)

Here's another connection! Frederick Douglass was an African American abolitionist, orator, and writer. What did Douglass want Reconstruction to achieve?

How did his goals for Reconstruction compare with those of others?

## Connect to the End of Reconstruction

**Lesson 4** New Restrictions on African American Rights
(See Student Text, page 577)

As troops withdrew from the South, what were some new ways that African Americans were prevented from exercising their rights?

Did Reconstruction successfully rebuild society?

It's Your Turn! **Find two more connections. Fill in the title of your connections, then answer the questions. Connections may be images, primary sources, maps, or text.**

# Your Choice | Connect to

## Location in text

What is the main idea of this connection?

What does this tell you about the events and legacy of Reconstruction?

# Your Choice | Connect to

## Location in text

What is the main idea of this connection?

What does this tell you about the events and legacy of Reconstruction?

**Examine Primary Sources** (See Student Text, page 580)

Examine the primary and secondary sources provided online or from your teacher. Fill in the chart to show how these sources provide further information about whether the United States should have ended Reconstruction in 1877. The first one is completed for you.

| Should the United States have ended Reconstruction in 1877? | |
|---|---|
| **Source** | **Yes or No? Why?** |
| **"Reconstruction Reassessed"** | YES, because freed slaves were unequipped to succeed with control of the corrupt southern government, making the South vulnerable to "Northern adventures." |
| **"The Supreme Court and the History of Reconstruction—and Vice-Versa"** | |
| **"The Use of Military Force to Protect the Gains of Reconstruction"** | |

**INTERACTIVE**

For extra help with Step 3, review the 21st Century Tutorial: **Compare Viewpoints**.

## ④ Discuss! (See Student Text, page 580)

Now that you have collected clues and explored documents about the end of Reconstruction, you are ready to discuss with your fellow historians the Guiding Question: **Should the United States have ended Reconstruction in 1877?** Follow the steps below, using the spaces provided to prepare for your discussion.

You will work with a partner in a small group of historians. Try to reach a consensus, a situation in which everyone is in agreement, on the question. Can you do it?

1. **Prepare Your Arguments** You will be assigned a position on the question, either YES or NO.

My position:

Work with your partner to review your Quest notes from the Quest Connections and Quest Sources.

- If you were assigned YES, agree with your partner on what you think were the strongest arguments from Godkin and Foner.

- If you were assigned NO, agree on what you think were the strongest arguments from Blair.

2. **Present Your Position** Those assigned YES will present their arguments and evidence first. As you listen, ask clarifying questions to gain information and understanding.

| What is a Clarifying Question? | |
|---|---|
| These types of questions do not judge the person talking. They are only for the listener to be clear on what he or she is hearing. | |
| Example: Can you tell me more about that? | Example: You said [x]. Am I getting that right? |

**INTERACTIVE**

For extra help with Step 4, review the 21st Century Tutorial: **Participate in a Discussion or Debate**.

While the opposite side speaks, take notes on what you hear in the space below.

3. **Switch!** Now NO and YES will switch sides. If you argued YES before, now you will argue NO. Work with your same partner and use your notes. Add any arguments and evidence from the clues and sources. Those *now* arguing YES go first.

When both sides have finished, answer the following:

| *Before* I started this discussion with my fellow historians, my opinion was that the United States | *After* this discussion with my fellow historians, my opinion is that the United States |
| --- | --- |
| _____should have ended Reconstruction in 1877. | _____should have ended Reconstruction in 1877. |
| _____should not have ended Reconstruction in 1877. | _____should not have ended Reconstruction in 1877. |

4. **Point of View** Do you all agree on the answer to the Guiding Question?

- _____Yes

- _____No

If not, on what points do you all agree?

# Take Notes

**Literacy Skills: Identify Cause and Effect** Use what you have read to complete the chart. Draw a line connecting the cause to the effect. The first one has been completed for you.

| Cause | Effect |
|-------|--------|
| Soldiers came home at the end of the war. | Environmental damage, including destruction of southern farms and forests, was widespread. |
| More battles took place in the South. | The Freedmen's Bureau was created to help with food, clothing, medical care, education, and jobs. |
| Freed African Americans needed help beginning new lives. | Many people were looking for jobs. |
| The Thirteenth Amendment banned slavery throughout the nation. | The South had to redefine its social and economic systems. |

**INTERACTIVE**

For extra help, review the 21st Century Tutorial: **Analyze Cause and Effect**.

# Practice Vocabulary

**Vocabulary Quiz Show**  Some quiz shows ask a question and expect the contestant to give the answer. In other shows, the contestant is given an answer and must supply the question. If the blank is in the Question column, write the question that would result in the answer in the Answer column. If the question is supplied, write the answer.

| **Question** | **Answer** |
| --- | --- |
| 1. What agency was established to help former slaves begin their new lives? | 1. |
| 2. What is a government pardon called? | 2. |
| 3. | 3. freedmen |
| 4. | 4. Thirteenth Amendment |
| 5. What name was given to describe the rebuilding of the nation? | 5. |

## Quick Activity Debate with a Partner

In the roles of Congressional Republicans in 1864, debate with your partner the Ten Percent Plan versus the Wade-Davis Bill. Summarize your main ideas in this table.

| Ten Percent Plan | Wade-Davis Bill |
| --- | --- |
| | |

**Team Challenge!** Reconstruction of the South was a long process. When Andrew Johnson became president, his plan for Reconstruction called for a majority of voters in each Southern state to pledge loyalty to the United States and to ratify the Thirteenth Amendment, which banned slavery throughout the nation. Discuss how Johnson's plan compared to the Ten Percent Plan and the Wade-Davis Bill. Given how Reconstruction played out, how might the adoption of one of these alternative plans have changed the course of events?

The Reconstruction Era

# Take Notes

**Literacy Skills: Identify Supporting Details** Use what you have read to complete the table. Respond to each main idea with two supporting details. The first one has been completed for you.

| Main Idea | Supporting Details |
|---|---|
| Even after the Thirteenth Amendment passed, the rights of African Americans were still extremely restricted. | • Under the black codes, freedmen were not allowed to vote, own guns, or serve on juries.<br><br>• In some states, freedmen were only permitted to work as servants or farm laborers. |
| Radical Republicans wanted to improve civil rights and equality. | |
| The Fourteenth Amendment was an important step toward civil rights. | |
| Congress and President Johnson disagreed on how to proceed with Reconstruction. | |
| After the passage of the Fifteenth Amendment, there was still a long way to go to achieve civil rights. | |

**INTERACTIVE**

For extra help, review the 21st Century Tutorial: **Support Ideas with Evidence**.

# Practice Vocabulary

**True or False?** Decide whether each statement below is true or false. Circle T or F, and then explain your answer. Be sure to include the underlined vocabulary word in your explanation. The first one is done for you.

1. **T / F** The <u>black codes</u> were laws to help freedmen build new lives. **False; The <u>black codes</u> were laws that severely restricted the rights of freed African Americans.**

2. **T / F** <u>Radical Republicans</u> wanted to ensure freedmen received the right to vote.

3. **T / F** The <u>Reconstruction Act</u> of 1867 accepted all of the states back into the Union.

4. **T / F** The <u>Fourteenth Amendment</u> defined citizens as "all persons born or naturalized in the United States."

5. **T / F** The House of Representatives voted to <u>impeach</u> President Johnson because they agreed with him.

6. **T / F** The <u>Fifteenth Amendment</u> gave African American men over the age of 21 the right to vote.

## Take Notes

**Literacy Skills: Summarize** Use what you have read to complete the table. In each box, list at least two details or ideas that describe the issue. Use your responses to summarize the lesson in three to five sentences. One has been completed for you.

| | |
|---|---|
| **New Political Groups** | • white southern republicans<br><br>• |
| **Conservatives Resist Reform** | |
| **Political Problems Slow Progress** | |
| **Economic Problems in the South** | |

**Summary**

**INTERACTIVE**

For extra help, review the 21st Century Tutorial: **Summarize**.

# Practice Vocabulary

**Sentence Builder** Finish the sentences below with a key term from this section. You may have to change the form of the words to complete the sentences.

## Word Bank

| | |
|---|---|
| Ku Klux Klan | carpetbagger |
| sharecropper | scalawag |

**1.** A Southerner who helped Southern Republicans was referred to as a

**2.** Northerners who moved to the South were often called

**3.** Someone who farms a rented plot of land is called a

**4.** The most dangerous group who terrorized African Americans is called the

# Take Notes

**Literacy Skills: Draw Conclusions** Use what you have read to complete the diagram. List ways that African Americans in the South were prevented from exercising their rights during this time. Then, make conclusions about the impact these restrictions had on these citizens. The first detail has been completed for you.

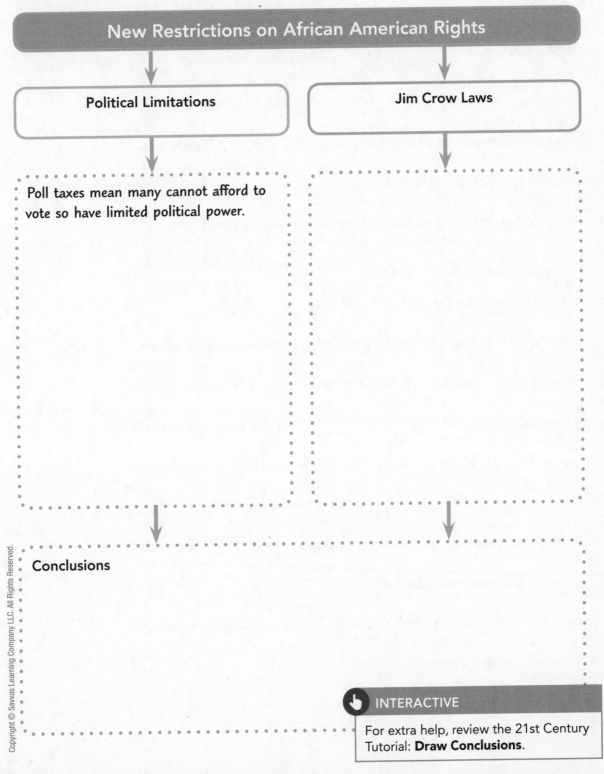

**New Restrictions on African American Rights**

| Political Limitations | Jim Crow Laws |
|---|---|
| Poll taxes mean many cannot afford to vote so have limited political power. | |

**Conclusions**

> **INTERACTIVE**
>
> For extra help, review the 21st Century Tutorial: **Draw Conclusions**.

## Practice Vocabulary

**Use a Word Bank** Choose one word from the word bank to fill in each blank. When you have finished, you will have a short summary of important ideas from the section.

### Word Bank

| | | |
|---|---|---|
| segregation | "New South" | poll tax |
| Compromise of 1877 | Jim Crow laws | *Plessy* v. *Ferguson* |
| literacy test | grandfather clause | |

With the :................................: and election of Rutherford B.

Hayes, Reconstruction ended. Laws to prevent African Americans from

exercising their rights included a :................................:, which

required voters to pay each time they voted. The laws also included

a :................................:, which required voters to read and

explain parts of the Constitution, and a :................................:

that stated if a voter's father or grandfather had been able to vote in

January 1867, then that voter did not have to take the literacy test.

After 1877, :................................:, or separation of the races,

became the law of the South. In 1896, the famous Supreme Court case

:................................: ruled that separate was legal as long

as facilities for blacks and whites were equal, even though they rarely

were. These laws were called the :................................:. As the

economy in the South started to change and improve for some people,

it became referred to as the :................................:.

# Quick Activity  Newspaper Editorial

Write a newspaper editorial supporting or opposing Samuel Tilden and the Democratic Party for choosing not to fight the commission's decision to award all of the disputed electors to Hayes. Use the chart below to help you organize your thinking.

## Did you know?

An editorial is an opinion piece that uses facts to support an argument.

**Introduction**
State your thesis.

**Evidence**
Support your claim with textual and factual evidence.

**Conclusion**
Help readers arrive at your conclusion based on the evidence you have provided.

**Team Challenge!** Find a partner with a different opinion. Share your charts and talk about the differences. Practice listening to your partner's reasoning without arguing or making statements of your own. Instead, limit your responses to questions that help you better understand your partner's perspective and that help your partner develop and refine his or her opinion.

# Writing Workshop Research Paper

As you read, build a response to the following research topic: **The Freedmen's Bureau, its effects, and the restrictions placed on the rights and opportunities of African Americans in the Reconstruction-era South.** The prompts below will help walk you through the process.

## Lesson 1 Writing Task: Generate Questions to Focus Research
(See Student Text, page 557)

At the end of this topic, you will write a research paper about the Freedmen's Bureau, its effects, and the restrictions placed on the rights and opportunities of African Americans in the Reconstruction-era South. Make a list of questions that would need to be answered in order to write a research paper on this subject, such as: What was the Freedmen's Bureau?

## Lesson 2 Writing Task: Find and Use Credible Sources
(See Student Text, page 563)

You will need more information to write your paper. List at least three credible sources of information you might use to research about the Freedmen's Bureau. Record the source information so you can find it again later.

## Lesson 3 Writing Task: Support Ideas with Evidence
(See Student Text, page 572)

A thesis is a statement that a writer intends to support and prove. Write a thesis statement for your research paper. Then, outline your research paper by writing your main ideas. Under each main idea, write facts and other evidence that support that idea.

**Thesis**

**Main Idea**

**Main Idea**

**Main Idea**

**Evidence**

**Evidence**

**Evidence**

## Lesson 4 Writing Task: Cite Sources (See Student Text, page 579)

Review the sources that you noted. Write citations for all of your sources, following the format provided by your teacher. Include the name of the article or text, the author, the publisher, the date of publication, and the web address (if applicable).

## Writing Task (See Student Text, page 581)

Complete your research paper on the Freedmen's Bureau and its effects. Include a discussion of the limits placed on African Americans. Your paper should include a strong conclusion that summarizes your thesis and main ideas.

# Acknowledgments

**Photography**

**COVER:**

CVR Shaunl/E+/Getty Images

**002** Mireille Vautier/Art Resource, NY; **004** Bjorn Landstrom/National Geographic/Getty Images; **005** Art Directors & TRIP/Alamy Stock Photo; **006** Mansa Kankan Musa I, 14th century king of the Mali empire (gouache on paper), McBride, Angus (1931–2007)/Private Collection/Look and Learn/Bridgeman Art Library; **007** Mikael Utterström/Alamy Stock Photo; **009** Greg Balfour Evans/Alamy Stock Photo; **010** Colport/Alamy Stock Photo; **011** PhotoStock-Israel/Alamy Stock; **024** North Wind Picture Archives/Alamy Stock Photo; **026** North Wind Picture Archives/Alamy Stock Photo; **028** Anonymous Person/AKG Images; **029** Courthouse, Philadelphia (oil on canvas), Smith, Russell William Thompson (1812–98)/Philadelphia History Museum at the Atwater Kent/Courtesy of Historical Society of Pennsylvania Collection/Bridgeman Art Library; **031** Marka/UIG/Getty Images; **033** Niday Picture Library/Alamy Stock Photo; **056** Archive Images/Alamy Stock Photo; **057** Digital Image Library/Alamy Stock Photo; **060** Vlad G/Shutterstock; **066** Archive Images/Alamy Stock Photo; **076** World History Archive/Alamy Stock Photo; **079** Culture Club/Getty Images; **080** Albert Knapp/Alamy Stock Photo; **081** Orhan Cam/Shutterstock; **083** Ken Cedeno/Corbis/Getty Images; **090** Hulton Archive/MPI/Getty Images; **099** Cartoonist Group; **104** North Wind Picture Archives/Alamy Stock Photo; **106** Orhan Cam/Shutterstock; **107** Carol M Highsmith/Library of Congress Prints and Photographs Division Washington [LC-DIG-highsm-09904]; **108** Science Source; **109** GL Archive/Alamy Stock Photo; **111** Lanmas/Alamy Stock Photo; **112** The Metropolitan Museum of Art/Art Resource, NY; **118** Library of Congress Prints and Photographs Division Washington [LC-DIG-ppmsca-31832]; **130** W H Jackson/MPI/Getty Images; **132T** Prisma Archivo/Alamy Stock Photo; **132B** Underwood Archives/Getty Images; **134** Carol M. Highsmith/Library of Congress Prints and Photographs Division [LC-DIG-highsm-27900]; **135** World History Archive/Alamy Stock Photo; **137** World History Archive/Alamy Stock Photo; **142** Heritage Image Partnership Ltd/Alamy Stock Photo; **155** Hulton Archive/Getty Images; **158** Niday Picture Library/Alamy Stock Photo; **160** UIG/Underwood Archives/Akg-images; **161** North Wind Picture Archives/Alamy Stock Photo; **162** Courtesy of the New York Public Library; **163** North Wind Picture Archives/Alamy Stock Photo; **165** Hulton Archive/Getty Images; **166** Picture History/Newscom; **167** American Anti-Slavery Society/Library of Congress Rare Book and Special Collections Division Washington [LC-USZC4-5321]; **176** Photo12/UIG/Getty Images; **184** John Parrot/Stocktrek Images/Alamy Stock Photo; **186** Katherine Frey/The Washington Post/Getty Images; **187** Everett Collection Inc/Alamy Stock Photo; **188** Abraham Lincoln (1809–65) in public debate with Stephen A. Douglas (1813–61) in Illinois, 1858 (colour litho), American School, (19th century)/Private Collection/Peter Newark American Pictures/Bridgeman Art Library; **189** The New York Historical Society/Getty Images; **191** H.Armstrong Roberts/ClassicStock/Alamy Stock Photo; **192** Abraham Lincoln with Allan Pinkerton and Major General John A. McClernand, 1862 (b/w photo), Gardner, Alexander (1821–82)/Collection of the New-York Historical Society, USA/Bridgeman Art Library; **193** Lawcain/Fotolia; **198** Jerry Pinkney/National Geographic Creative/Alamy Stock Photo; **210** LOC Photo/Alamy Stock Photo; **213** Charles Sumner (1811–74), US Senator; photo by George Warren, Boston (albumen print), American Photographer, (19th century)/American Antiquarian Society, Worcester, Massachusetts, USA/Bridgeman Art Library; **214** Lightfoot/Getty Images; **215** Universal Images Group North America LLC/Encyclopaedia Britannica, Inc./Library of Congress/Alamy Stock Photo; **217** MPI/Getty Images; **219** Artokoloro Quint Lox Limited/Alamy Stock Photo.